ALL IN A DAY'S RIDING

TERRITORY OF NEW MEXICO
1880s

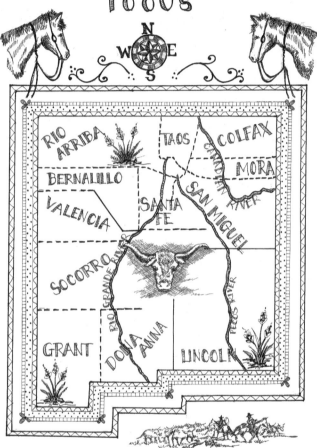

Map courtesy of Shari Zimmer
ZZ Bar Ranch, Cimarron, NM

ALL IN A DAY'S RIDING

STORIES OF THE NEW MEXICO RANGE
COMPILED WITH INTRODUCTORY ESSAYS

By

STEPHEN ZIMMER

SUNSTONE
PRESS

SANTA FE

Special thanks to Gene Lamm of Cimarron, New Mexico for his
exceptional work in preparing the illustrations for publication.

Sunstone books may be purchased for educational, business, or sales promotional use.
For information please write: Special Markets Department, Sunstone Press,
P.O. Box 2321, Santa Fe, New Mexico 87504-2321.

Design › R. Ahl
Printed on acid-free paper
∞
eBook 978-1-61139-638-6

_____

Library of Congress Cataloging-in-Publication Data

Names: Zimmer, Stephen, author.
Title: All in a day's riding : stories of the New Mexico range, compiled
    with introductory essays / Stephen Zimmer.
Description: Santa Fe, New Mexico : Sunstone Press, [2021] | Includes
    bibliographical references. | Summary: "A collection of stories from the
    works of Western writers with introductory essays by Stephen Zimmer"--
    Provided by publisher.
Identifiers: LCCN 2021058870 | ISBN 9781632933607 (paperback) | ISBN
    9781611396386 (epub) | ISBN 1632933608 (paperback)
Subjects: LCSH: Frontier and pioneer life--New Mexico--Anecdotes. |
    Ranching--New Mexico--Anecdotes. | Cowboys--New Mexico--Anecdotes.
Classification: LCC F796.6 .Z56 2021 | DDC 978.9/02--dc23/eng/20211214
LC record available at https://lccn.loc.gov/2021058870

_____

WWW.SUNSTONEPRESS.COM
SUNSTONE PRESS / POST OFFICE BOX 2321 / SANTA FE, NM 87504-2321 /USA
(505) 988-4418

DEDICATION
For riders of the New Mexico Range, yesterday and today

Contents

Foreword
David L. Caffey

Eugene Manlove Rhodes, one of the writers featured in this volume, had a long running frustration with writers and publishers who, he said, gave the public a steady, gushing torrent of misinformation about the American West and the people who lived and worked there in the late nineteenth century. As a writer, he concentrated on those he knew best: cowboys and cattlemen, miners, and some among the few women who inhabited that world. Rhodes had a deep sense of obligation to truth in his portrayals of people he wrote about, their experiences, and their values. At the same time, his western tales were works of fiction, meant to entertain as well as enlighten readers of the Saturday Evening Post and other popular periodicals of his early twentieth century era. He blamed the moguls of the mass print media for miseducating generations of readers about the West that was. His unyielding commitment was to serve honest portrayals, based on his own experience as a young man working out on the open range in the mountain and desert country of southern New Mexico, with men whose ability and work ethic had won his admiration. William H. Hutchinson, Rhodes's most attentive scholar and critic, characterized his identity as a writer as follows: "Fidelity to time and place and incident, fidelity to his land and its people and their values—this fidelity was Rhodes's hallmark."

The same desire to convey authentic and credible portrayals of the western cattle range and its people in its formative years, guided Steve Zimmer in choosing to collect and illuminate real, remembered experiences of times and places in the West that was. If the aim is an authentic depiction of cowboys, cowgirls, and early western cattle ranching, how better to find it than by consulting the testimonies and recollections of people who were there and took part in the great western migration, or who just lived lives on horseback, caring for animals, fixing fence, taking in wide and beautiful spaces and knowing the satisfaction of hard work well done? This is what may be said of those whose writings are related in this collection. The stories the writers tell are from their own experience, or as told to them by contemporaries.

At first glance, it seems an irony that the toil of a cowboy is at once hard and demanding, yet so cherished and appreciated by those who feel themselves fortunate to have lived the life. C. L. Sonnichsen, an Iowan by birth but a discerning student of all things western, finds the element of violence in western film and fiction much overdrawn, pointing out that most of the troubles of men engaged in cattle raising in the early West were nonviolent: "isolation, loneliness, boredom, backbreaking toil, mortgages, grasshoppers, blizzards, drouths, sickness, and old age and death." Quite a load. Funny, then, that so many have loved it so much. Elliott "Chope" Phillips grew up spending summers on his father's Philmont Ranch, and had near unlimited choices for education and career, but he found his passion working with a cow outfit amid the high summer pastures of the Cimarron country. "To be part of that was a wonderful experience," he recalled; "I guess it spoiled me for any other line of work." By choice, he spent his life ranching at Valmora, near the village of Watrous and old Fort Union.

Though the cowhand's usual work brought him in contact with many more range animals than people, the men of extraordinary character and skill encountered doing range work made for some of the most memorable impressions. Jack Culley, whose story of wild cattle and horses will be found in these pages, was born in England, but found a home in the American West, spending his best years as a ranch hand and manager on ranches in eastern New Mexico. After years in the cattle business and others spent in contemplation of his experiences, Culley could say, "Allowing for occasional differences, I never knew such a sense of true comradeship as ours was." Culley, like his brother and sometime riding partner, Chris, saw that "no man could ever have ridden the ranges and worked with these boys, without being a whole lot better for it. It brought out all that was best in a man, and made him ashamed of the more common weaknesses."

We can take the late Texas writer Larry McMurtry's word for it that the cattle range of yesteryear had its restless and brooding types. If Steve Zimmer shows a prejudice in his choice of first-hand narratives from the western range, it is for accounts of and about men and women who exemplify the better nature that was so often revealed in the tough and punishing work that ranch hands did and still do, albeit with the assistance of video cameras, cell phones, all-terrain vehicles and other additions to the more traditional tools of the trade. Their business has changed, and will continue to change, but there is still so much to be learned from those who came before.

"It is estimated that fully 95 per cent of the lands of Western Dakota, Western Nebraska, Montana, Wyoming, Utah, Arizona, New Mexico, and Colorado is, on account of the small amount of precipitation, capable of producing only bunch grass, gramma, buffalo grass, and other nutritious grasses, fit only for the pasturage of animals. The fact of limited rain fall that occurs mainly during the spring and summer months appears to be the essential condition to the production of these grasses.

"Its value for pasturage is dependent on a reasonable proximity to water. It is found that range cattle can graze to advantage only on lands situated within six or seven miles of water. The result is that throughout the range cattle area grazing is limited mainly to strips of land from 12 to14 miles in width along streams of water."

—Joseph Nimmo, Jr., *The Range and Ranch Cattle Traffic in the Western States* 1885

"When I started running cattle (northeastern New Mexico, late 1880s), there wasn't a vestige of a fence around the house I lived in. Straight from my very doorstep ran the open road to Arizona, Montana, Texas, Nevada, or Wyoming. Your cattle might stray off to a point a thousand miles away from their home range. But there were means through brand books and a system of advertising to restore them to you or dispose of them for you. The occupants of the vast cattle range country during the range cattle period constituted a kind of fraternity, loose but cooperative in certain important purposes of life, on a scale such as the world had never seen and may never see again."

—Jack Culley, *Cattle, Horses, and Men*

THE NEW MEXICO CATTLE FRONTIER
1865–1900

"The profits of stock raising in this Western country are so great that should I tell the truth, it might be taken as an exaggeration."
—Journalist C.M. Chase of Vermont during a visit to Colfax County, New Mexico in 1881

Cattle were first introduced into present-day New Mexico in 1598 by the Spanish colonizer Don Juan Onate. His settlers also drove herds of sheep which became the colonists' preferred domestic animal not only for their meat, but wool as well. For the next three and a half centuries sheep prospered on the mountains, mesas, and plains that surrounded the Spanish settlements along the Rio Grande despite frequent raids by Apache and Navajo Indians. Cattle were of less importance as a food source, and most of the bovines that ranged their ranchos were used as draft oxen.

Cattle grazing did not become economically important until after the New Mexican province was acquired by the United States and made a Territory in 1846 at the beginning of the Mexican War. The first American cattle raiser was Lucien B. Maxwell, a former mountain man and trader, who colonized a settlement on the Beaubien and Miranda Land Grant in the northeastern part of the Territory in 1848. Maxwell first grazed work oxen that he bartered to traders traveling the Santa Fe Trail but later built-up vast herds of beef cattle on his ranch on the Cimarron River that he sold to troops stationed at Fort Union sixty miles to the south. Later he supplied the Jicarilla and Ute tribes with beef when their reservation agency was established at his ranch in 1861.

The first non-native cattle introduced into New Mexico came from Texas when Charles Goodnight and Oliver Loving drove a mixed herd of Longhorn cows and steers to the Pecos River in July of 1866. They sold the steers to the military at Fort Sumner and the nearby Navajo

Agency at Bosque Redondo. Goodnight immediately returned to Texas for another herd and arrived at the Bosque late in the year. Because the fort and agency had little need of cattle at that time, Goodnight wintered the herd on the Pecos and sold more than 1300 head to beef contractors early in the spring.

John S. Chisum followed Goodnight in 1866 with a herd of steers reaching the Bosque in December. After selling the steers to the government he returned to Texas for another herd. For the next three years Goodnight and Chisum partnered on cattle that Chisum piloted from Texas to the Pecos River. What cattle they were unable to sell Goodnight drove north to Colorado and either sold in mining camps or to cattlemen who were stocking the eastern ranges of the Territory.

Chisum remained on the Pecos and eventually built-up immense herds that ranged south to the Texas border. Aside from selling beef to Indian reservations he also supplied various forts around the Territory and southern Arizona. By the time of his death in 1884 he was known as the "Cattle King of New Mexico."

Economic conditions changed dramatically in New Mexico when the Atchison, Topeka, and Santa Fe Railroad laid tracks into the Territory over Raton Pass in the fall of 1879. The line ran south to Las Vegas and then to Albuquerque on the Rio Grande. Eventually, it intersected the Southern Pacific Railroad at Deming in the southern part of the Territory where it proceeded west to California. The Santa Fe provided transportation for cattle to slaughterhouses in Kansas City and Chicago that had been established to supply processed beef to the burgeoning population of the industrial United States.

As a result, cattlemen from Texas started driving large herds of Longhorns onto New Mexico's public domain in order to take advantage of the nutritious grama grass that blanketed more than half of the Territory. Many of the herds which were composed of bulls, cows, calves, and beef steers in various proportions were owned by corporate entities headquartered in the Mid-West, East, or Great Britain. From 1882 to 1886 one hundred and four cattle companies were incorporated in New Mexico with a total capitalization of twenty-three million dollars. Some of the outfits, such as the Prairie Cattle Company (Cross L), the Dubuque Cattle Company (Bar T Cross), and the Maxwell Cattle Company (Long H) ran as many as 20,000 head. In addition, there were several individuals who put together large operations including Stephen

Dorsey (Triangle Dot), George Littlefield (LFD), Tom Lyons and Angus Campbell (L-C) and Wilson Waddingham (Bell Ranch).

Interspersed among the big outfits were numerous individuals who filed claims on 160-acre tracts of the public domain under the Homestead Act of 1862. Generally, these "small fellows" located on perennial streams where their cattle could water, yet still graze over a wide area. After recording a brand, these cattlemen usually ran herds of under one thousand head.

Albert Thompson was a typical homestead rancher. Early in 1886 he filed on 160 acres on Pinavetitos Creek twenty miles from present day Clayton, New Mexico. On his claim he built a "stone house, 12 feet square with a fireplace in one corner and a dirt roof and floor," with one door and one window. He furnished his camp with "a rough board table, a box fastened to the wall which served as a cupboard, a dutch oven, frying pan and coffee pot, and a couple of rudely made stools." A camp bed rolled up by day and spread out on the floor at night completed his domestic arrangements. Thompson acquired a few head of cattle and recorded a brand but also joined the adjoining Lake Cattle Company on their spring and fall works to supplement his income.

The rising number of Longhorns grazing the New Mexico range after 1880 reflected the Santa Fe's impact. In Colfax Country, which comprised the far northeast quadrant of the Territory, 200,000 sheep and only 75,000 head of cattle grazed the county in 1875. Ten years later the number of cattle had increased to nearly 500,000 head. At the same time Lincoln County boasted 400,000 head while Dona Ana County counted almost 350,000 head. The high numbers were a direct result of the greater amount of live water in these counties as compared with other counties located in more arid environments.

The price per head also increased. In 1879 cattle sold for $7 per head, while two years later the price had jumped to $12.00. By 1884 the price of a beef steer in Chicago was at a high of $24.00. As a result, many cattlemen began overstocking the range in order to take advantage of the high price.

With so many outfits working the range cattlemen recognized the value of working cooperatively and did so by forming stock growers' associations designed to promote their common interests. The Northern New Mexico Stock Growers' Association, headquartered in Springer, along with similar organizations in Lincoln and Dona Ana Counties were among such groups established in the early 1880s. Each association issued a brand book that listed its membership which included owners of as few as one hundred head to big outfits that grazed over 20,000. Primarily the associations organized annual roundups and sought to combat cattle rustling which had become rampant throughout the Territory. Importantly, they also lobbied the Santa Fe and later other railroads for lower shipping rates.

The associations all had similar concerns. In 1885 O.A. Hadley, president of the Northern New Mexico Association addressed a typical one when he warned his members against allowing "the usual fast riding of horses and driving of cattle by employees on the annual roundups" because it was not only unnecessary, but harmful to the stock as well. In addition, his association, like others, established a rule that prohibited "habitual carrying of pistols by employees of its members."

With so many cattle on the open range herds invariably strayed and mixed with cattle from other outfits. In order to separate them and return them to their home ranges, two annual roundups were conducted. The first began in the spring once the grass began to green. Initiated by the big outfits, roundups involved sending cowboys crews over the country where cattle had drifted during the winter. Representatives from other outfits including the smaller neighbors were invited to participate so they could also return their strays. During this roundup, the cowboys branded the calves that had been born in the spring.

Each roundup was accompanied by a cook and chuck wagon that provided meals for the crew and carried their beds and camp equipment. Sometimes a roundup wagon would make a circle of more than one hundred miles and be out for three or four months before making its way back to the outfit's headquarters. Often the larger outfits would send out more than one wagon in order to cover an even greater area.

Once back at the ranch the wagon was resupplied, and the horses were re-shod. The outfits then headed out again this time to gather the three and four-year old marketable beef steers that would be driven to the nearest Santa Fe railroad shipping point such as Springer and Las Vegas in the north and Engle and Deming in the south. In 1887 the Denver & Ft. Worth railroad was built through the far northeast corner of the Territory. The town of Clayton was established on the line and soon became popular with drovers.

The challenges of running cattle on New Mexico's open range

were many. The semi-arid environment often brought succeeding years of drought where little snow fell in winter and the same for rain in summer. On the other hand, some winters were excessively cold and wet which caused the loss of all classes of cattle especially breeding bulls. Wolves were an additional threat to herds as they preyed on Longhorn cattle instead of buffalo that had been hunted out of the southern Great Plains in the 1870s. The Maxwell Cattle Company that ranged Lucien Maxwell's old land grant had the additional problem of having to deal with settlers who illegally grazed cattle on its land.

Some outfits dealt with homesteaders and small ranchers by erecting barbed wire fences in order to keep them from encroaching on their range. Nonetheless, the Territorial legislature voted against fencing the public domain and enacted a law in 1885 that made it not only an illegal act but a punishable one as well.

Slowly, the large outfits came to see the necessity of purchasing the grass they used in order to protect it. In addition, cattlemen recognized the desirability of upgrading their herds and began importing bulls from England such as Durhams (Shorthorns) and Herefords that produced the higher quality of beef with more fat demanded by consumers in the East.

It followed then that they began fencing their deeded pastures in order to better take care of their cattle. Simultaneously, they grew hay to feed their herds in the winter when the summer native grass had been consumed. They also drilled water wells on ranges devoid of surface water. For example, after the LFD outfit moved cattle onto the Llano Estacado plains east of the Pecos River in 1883, they drilled wells every ten miles so that their cattle could more efficiently graze the grass on the range.

In order to take advantage of the high market price in the early 1880s, many New Mexican cattlemen overstocked their ranges like operators from Texas to Montana were also doing. Over the winter of 1884-1885, however, prices dropped dramatically in Chicago after cattlemen flooded the market with surplus cattle that did not have sufficient grass. Consequently, many corporate outfits, crippled by declining revenues, were unable to pay the dividends due their investors and were forced out of business.

Some big outfits like the Prairie Cattle Company, the Bell Ranch, and the LFDs survived, however, by buying their range, fencing it, and stocking it with well-bred cattle. Most, on the other hand, liquidated and saw their former range divided among smaller ranchers and homesteaders. The days of great herds of Texas Longhorns grazing the New Mexico range were to be no more.

Lucien B. Maxwell of the Cimarron.

Jicarilla Apache beef and grain ration day at Maxwell's Aztec Mill at Cimarron, 1860s.

John S. Chisum, "The Cattle King of New Mexico."

Roundup outfit at the foot of the Wagon Mound, Territory of New Mexico, ca. 1885.

Typical New Mexican roundup outfit in camp. The cooks stands next to his wagon and chuck box. The cowboys often slept overnight in canvas range teepees.

Cross L cowboys branding calves on the open range.

Branding on the southern New Mexico range. Wood to heat the branding irons was gathered from the nearest creek bottom and hauled to the roundup ground. (New Mexico State University Library, Archives and Special Collections)

Cross L roundup outfit ready to leave from the Prairie Cattle Company's headquarters on the Dry Cimarron River.

Crow Creek headquarters, Maxwell Cattle Company, Colfax County. The structure still stands.

Maxwell Cattle Company (Long H) roundup crew, Maxwell Land Grant, 1892.

Cowboys gathered to pay their respects at the open range funeral of a fellow rider, George Brenton, who drowned crossing a creek during spring roundup, Prairie Cattle Company, 1891.

DUBUQUE CATTLE CO.

T. H. LAWRENCE, Manager.

P. O., LAS VEGAS, N. M.

RANGE—Tequesquite, Ute and Tremperson, Arroyas, Colfax and Mora Counties.

ADDITIONAL BRANDS.

OO JD O-D ED JOE AD HC ILL MC

All calves branded same as in cut.

HORSE BRAND, **EX** on left hip, **T** on left hip or shoulder.

MAXWELL CATTLE CO.

M. M. CHASE, Manager.

RANGE—Maxwell Grant, Colfax Co., N. M.

P. O., CIMARRON, N. M.

ADDITIONAL BRANDS.

Some cattle branded same as in cut, on right side and hip.

 on right side.

 on right side, **R** on right thigh.

HUHU on left side, ear mark, crop and split, the left.

KLM on left shoulder, side and hip.

PALO BLANCO CATTLE CO.

S. W. DORSEY, Manager.

P. O., CHICO SPRINGS, N. M.

RANGE—Currumpa, Palo Blanco, Ute Creek, Don Car-

THE PRAIRIE CATTLE CO. (Limited.)

R. G. HEAD, Manager, Trinidad, Colo.

PHLEM HUMPHRY, Ranch Supt.

P. O., TRINIDAD, COLO.

RANCH P. O., CATALPA, N. M.

RANGE—Colfax Co., N. M.

ADDITIONAL BRANDS.

7 7 TXT T-I J JL 7 I4 77 XT

HI J T- III HE A-L E-L

HORSE BRAND, same as principal brand on left shoulder or thigh.

WADDINGHAM BELL RANCH.

MICHAEL SLATTERY, Manager.

P. O., LA CINTA, SAN MIGUEL CO., N. M.

RANGE—Montoya Grant.

HORSE BRAND, same as cut, on left shoulder

LAKE RANCH CATTLE CO.

D. C. HOLCOMB, Manager.

P. J. TOWNER, Foreman.

P. O., CHICO SPRINGS, N. M.

RANGE—Ute Creek, Tramperos, Alamositas, and Carrizo, Mora Co., N. M.

Brands of some of the larger outfits who were members of the Northern New Mexico Stock Growers Association, northeastern New Mexico, 1884.

JESUS G. ABREU.

P. O., SPRINGER, N. M.

RANGE--Rayado.

CHASE, DAWSON & MAULDING.

P. O., CIMARRON, N. M.

RANGE--Vermejo and Poniel.

MAXWELL CATTLE CO.

M. M. CHASE, Manager.

RANGE—Maxwell Grant, Colfax Co., N. M.

H. M. PORTER.

P. O., DENVER, COLO.

RANGE--Uraca, Cimarron.

M. HECK.

P. O., CIMARRON, N. M.

RANGE--Cimarroncito and Canon Bonito.

MARION LITTRELL.

P. O., VERMEJO, N. M.

RANGE—Vermejo, Red River and Teneja.

Cimarron area outfits, Northern New Mexico Stock Growers Association brand book, 1884.

A horse wrangler experiences difficulty with his mount during a roundup. Wranglers were generally young, inexperienced hands who herded the remuda, the Spanish word for the cowboys' horses.

A roundup crew eating at noon which was referred to as dinner. The cook prepared meals in cast iron dutch ovens. All three daily meals consisted of beef, either roasted or stewed, accompanied by sourdough biscuits and boiled coffee. Canned corn or tomatoes, when available, were cowboy favorites. (New Mexico State University Library, Archives and Special Collections)

Cowboys roping their mounts for the morning gather.

Prairie Cattle Company JJ Arkansas River Division. The majority of riders on the New Mexico and southern Colorado range were from Texas. A good number of them were African American.

Representatives from several outfits located along the Dry Cimarron River including the 101s, the ZHs, and the Cross Ls, 1889. All three outfits were financed by Scottish syndicates.

Roundup outfit saddled and ready to move camp. The cowboys' beds are rolled and carried in the wagon bed. Wagons were pulled by two spans (pairs) of either horses or mules.

Roundup rep with his bed lashed to a grey horse.

A roundup crew stopped at noon for dinner. Many cowboys wore wool suit coats and vests for the benefit of extra pockets to hold tobacco and cigarette papers, money, a pencil and a small notebook among other things. (New Mexico State University Library, Archives and Special Collections)

A group of cowpunchers who have roped a steer probably in anticipation of a BBQ. Springer, Territory of New Mexico.

A Hispanic cowpuncher from the southern New Mexican range ca. 1890s. Cowboys used ropes to drag calves for branding, rope horses, and catch cattle on the open range. Some ropes were made from twisted sisal hemp while others were of braided rawhide. (New Mexico State Library University Library, Archives and Special Collections)

A trail crew camped by a playa lake outside of the Santa Fe Railroad shipping yards at Springer. Most men wore grey colored hats made from beaver fur while others preferred black.

Two cowpunchers from the southern New Mexican range. The rider on the right is wearing leather leggings or chaps. Both ride Great Plains saddles, popular in Texas and the Southwest, that featured square skirts, a high cantle (back), and a horn in front that was used to tie the end of the rope when roping. (New Mexico State University Library, Archives and Special Collections)

A New Mexico range outfit from the southern part of the Territory, ca 1890s. (New Mexico State University Library, Archives and Special Collections)

This roundup crew is using a wagon purchased from the Springer Mercantile and Building Company, Territory of New Mexico, ca. 1890s. Cowboys slept in heavy canvas bed tarps while on roundup. The tarps usually measured 7' x 18' and were folded lengthwise with blankets placed in between.

Riders and Writers of the New Mexico Range

"Speakin' of cowpunchers," says Rawhide Rawlins, "I'm glad to see in the last few years that them that know the business have been writin' about'em. It begin to look like they'd be wiped out without a history."
—Charles Russell, *Trails Plowed Under*

"The daily life of the cowboy is so replete with privation, hardship, and danger that it is a marvel how any sane man can voluntarily assume it. Yet thousands of men not only do assume it, but actually like it to infatuation."
—Richard Irving Dodge, 1882

Several men and women who rode the New Mexico range in the 1880s and '90s left recollections about the life they experienced. Ten of them are represented here with excerpts from the books they wrote. Together their writings provide a vivid glimpse into what it was like to take care of cattle and horses on the New Mexico range before it was fenced. Unfortunately, many New Mexico cowpunchers, like those on other cattle ranges, could neither read nor write and so were unable to write about the work they did and their fellow "hired men on horseback." But the accounts that do exist are instructive in helping the modern reader appreciate conditions as they were on the New Mexico cattle frontier at the end of the 19th Century.

The authors represented here came from many backgrounds. Only one was born in New Mexico, and only one came from Texas. The others came either from the Mid-West, East Coast, or the British Isles, and the diversity of their origins was like those of ranchmen on other cattle frontiers. By and large, most of them learned how to handle cows and horses once they arrived on the cattle range. In other words, they learned to punch cows by punching cows.

Most of them wrote their stories in their twilight years when the lapse of time had softened the often-harsh reality of riding on the range when they were forced to work during blizzards, wind storms, floods, and droughts. While most of the entries are devoted to normal cow work, there are also more dramatic accounts of contending with stampedes, riding bucking horses, fending off angry bulls, or protecting themselves against raiding Indians.

Despite the strenuous work and often low pay, one gets the feeling that all the authors would have rather been horseback on the range than working in a steel mill, mining coal, or chopping cotton. As one of them, James Cook, wrote, "when the weather was fine, and we had plenty of rest and food, I enjoyed cowboy life thoroughly, and at such time, would not have exchanged places with the Prince of Wales."

Cover of C.M. Chase's book, *The Editor's Run in New Mexico and Colorado.*

C.M. Chase

C.M. Chase was editor of a newspaper in Vermont. In October of 1881 he traveled to New Mexico Territory to visit his cousin, Manly M. Chase, who ranched on the Ponil River outside of Cimarron. Manly Chase was born in 1842 in Wisconsin and moved with his family at age sixteen to Colorado during the gold rush there. After marrying, he moved south to the Maxwell Land Grant in northeastern New Mexico and began ranching on the Vermejo River.

In 1869 he traded a herd of horses to Lucien Maxwell for one thousand acres on the land grant on the Ponil River north of Cimarron. Subsequently he either managed or was part owner in several cattle and sheep outfits in the Territory including the Maxwell Cattle Company, along with the Cimarron, Gila, and Red River Cattle Companies. His cousin had come to New Mexico to investigate the profitability of investing in livestock raising and eventually put money into all the enterprises that his cousin managed.

During his six-week visit, Chase wrote twenty-eight essay letters to his home newspaper that were later compiled under the title, *The Editor's Run in New Mexico and Colorado*. In the excerpt that follows, he projects phenomenal profits one could expect by investing in the range cattle business in the Territory of New Mexico. His analysis held true for the next few years until cattle prices dropped due to overcrowded ranges all over the Western cattle country and the subsequent sale of excess cattle in the Chicago and Kansas City markets.

The Editor's Run in New Mexico and Colorado
Fort Davis, Texas, Frontier Book Company, 1968
"Cimarron, New Mexico, October 18, 1881"

On arriving here last Saturday evening we found S.M. Folsom, who left Lyndonville (VT) three weeks ago, stopping at the residence of M.M. Chase, taking his first lesson in cattle raising. Before embarking extensively in the cattle business, Folsom concluded to devote a season to learning the business and has shown discretion in securing one of the most successful stock men in the country for an instructor.

Mr. Chase is a man 45 years old, and a border life experience of 30 years has given him the best qualifications for stock raising in a new country. Mr. Chase was born in Wisconsin, and his father, W.C. Chase, a native of Bradford, VT, being an extensive stockbroker, put him into the business of handling stock early in life. Before Colorado had made much pretension as a territory even, M.M. emigrated to the far West and took a hand in corralling Indians, hunting game, mining, etc. His business took him over a large part of the country from the Black Hills to Santa Fe, New Mexico. For a number of years he was engaged in the freighting business across the Plains, from the Missouri River to Denver. Some 15 years ago, being well acquainted with the greater portion of the range along the foothills of the Rocky Mountains, he selected Cimarron, N.M. as the finest climate he knew, and as a locality affording the richest range and the best shelter for cattle. He moved here, commenced to farm and start his herd. From a small beginning he has worked his way up to be the leading stock man in these parts. He has a residence three miles from Cimarron village, in a rich canon, from a half mile to a mile wide. His home place contains 1,000 acres of land. Here he keeps some 40 horses and about 300 head of cattle. The horses are designed mainly for his individual and family driving, and the cattle are the property of his children, who have them branded with their own marks. Fifteen miles to the north he and two partners, named Dawson and Maulding, have a ranch of 50,000 acres, all enclosed, about 20 miles of it having wire fence and 15 miles the walls of mountains. This range takes the natural drainage of the Vermejo River, is sufficient for 3,000 cattle and is already stocked with a herd of 2,500. This range is about half open prairie, the other half extending back into the foothills which contain numerous canons and mesas, largely covered with piñon trees, forming the finest imaginable shelter for cattle. The ranch is considered a sort of "home pasture," and is about eight by ten miles in extent. The canons extend way back into the foothills, forming beautiful parks, little and big, from 100 to 2000 acres in extent, dotted here and there with the piñons, and are as beautiful and romantic as it is possible to form on the bosom of Mother Earth. They are simply charming, and one almost envies the life of an animal in the possession of such homes. The hills rise up suddenly out of the flat land and terminate in flat tops, miles in extent and rich in grazing capacity. Though very steep and covered with piñons, most of their sides also form good grazing.

Mr. Chase and his partner Dawson own a sheep ranch 180 miles southeast of Cimarron, some 12 x 15 miles in extent which contains a greater number of acres than the "home pasture." This ranch is now stocked with 15,000 sheep of improved breed.

With the two partners above mentioned and three others, Mr. Chase purchased last year a tract of country 150 miles southeast of Cimarron and just north of the sheep ranch embracing about 60 x 13 miles in extent containing in round numbers 500,000 acres. This ranch is now stocked with 12,000 cattle and will range 50,000 allowing ten acres to each animal. In ordinary seasons this is sufficient. The company, however, intends to allow the herd to grow by purchase and increase to 25,000 head and then make their calculations for the future.

In addition to the above, Mr. Chase and his partner Dawson, Mr. Folsom, and four others, have purchased a tract of about 150,000 acres, 35 miles southeast of Cimarron, which has not been stocked as yet, but will be this winter by purchase of stock from Texas. It will range easily 10,000 to 15,000 head. Mr. Chase has the management of these different ranges, that is, he does the buying and selling and has general supervision, with a boss on each ranch, to attend to all details such as hiring the necessary help to ride the fence—go around the range daily to keep the fence in repair—round up the cattle at stated seasons, to cut out beef to be sold, calves to be branded, etc., For his supervision he gets a salary from each company in addition to his share of the profits.

In a former letter I spoke of the Maxwell Cattle Company, just formed for the purpose of stocking all the land in the Maxwell grant not yet disposed of, the number of acres being about 1,700,000. Mr. Sherwin, who holds 66 percent of the stock in this company and about the same of stock in the Maxwell Land Company, controls them both and will allow no more land to be sold or leased out of the grant, and he designs to have the cattle company stock all the land controlled by the Maxwell Land Company. The intention virtually puts an end to the increase of settlements in the grazing section of the Maxwell grant and holds it as a cattle grazing locality purely. Any future increase must come from the developments of the gold, silver, iron, copper and coal mines which are abundant in the hills. Mr. Chase has been engaged to manage the affairs of the Maxwell Cattle Company for five years, receiving therefore a liberal compensation annually, with a promise of a better situation at the end of that time. The salaries he receives for the management of different companies will, if he is prudent, keep his family from starvation. In a subsequent communication I will give particulars of the profits of sheep and cattle raising from which it will appear that he is in condition to lay by something for a rainy day.

Sunday was the first day spent in Cimarron, but it was so far gone when I discovered it that it was impossible to observe the Sabbath in the New England way. As a general rule, all days are alike here. There have been some attempts to support a minister in Cimarron and a little house has been built for one to expound his opinions in. But the first minister was shot, the second one was put in jail, while the third one got frightened and ran away. No man has since ventured publicly to expound the scripture to the Cimarron people. The church has been converted into a school house where it is proposed to educate the children and let them search the scriptures for themselves and parents.

This is a country of magnificent distances, and I have been bewildered ever since my arrival in attempting to comprehend the circuit of the neighborhood. When M.M. invited us to ride to his pasture, I asked him where it was, and he said "over here a little piece," pointing with his finger. I rode over with him and found it fifteen miles distant. That is what they call "a little piece." The next neighbor is usually five or ten miles distant. Localities 60 or 100 miles off are spoken of with the same neighborly familiarity that a Lyndon Corner man speaks of Lyndonville. This will account for the number of horses all prominent ranch men keep. M.M. lives three and one-half miles from the post office and has the first establishment out of the village. Twenty of his horses are used for his own and family roadsters, a part for odd jobs of teaming, and others are grazing on the home place and getting on age and condition for service. One span is used today, another tomorrow, and so on.

On Monday last we made our first trip out. Chase, Folsom, the Governor and myself rode over to H.M. Porter's pasture ten miles away to witness a "round up." The cattle in this pasture, about 2000 in number, are under the charge of cowboy George M. Chase who lived in Lyndon some 30 years ago. Realizing the profits of stock raising in New Mexico, he came here from Kansas City a year ago and engaged as a cowboy for H.M. Porter's herd. He determined to learn the business from the bottom up. The business of the cowboy is to live on the ranch with the cattle, ride along the fence every day to repair all breaks, see that the cattle are kept within their range, etc. George's enclosure fence is 30 miles in circumference, and he rides around it on horseback every day. In addition to his salary for service, he was allowed to put a few animals of his own. These animals he has just sold, nearly doubling his money inside of a year. On arriving at the pasture at three o'clock in the afternoon, we had several miles to ride before reaching the locality of the round up. We found the bunch, having been collected—rounded up—during the day by eight men on horseback. A part of the men were riding round the herd, keeping them bunched up, while the others were riding in and driving out of the herd particular animals wanted and driving them away to some place distant from the main herd, to sell, to brand, or for some other purpose. This process is called "cutting out."

On Tuesday the same quartette of individuals took another span of horses and drove north to Chase's Vermejo pasture. On the way we called at a place in the prairie where M.M. and his partner John Dawson have a band of sheep, 2,500 in number which had been cut out of the main flock to send to market.

On leaving the sheep camp, a mile ride over the prairie brought us to the wire fence of the home pasture—a fence 16 miles long. An opening was made, and we passed in, rode two miles, and came to the old Santa Fe station, now used as the home for Marion Littrell, the boss of the ranch. From here we passed on through the pasture over lonely country, entered a canon and passed up two miles to where the mountains draw together and form a canon a half mile wide. Here we found the residence of Mr. Dawson, a one story adobe house with adobe barn and adobe corral. Half of the house had been torn away and an addition was about to be built, but two or three small rooms were left. Dawson and wife, seven children, the school marm, and a visiting gentleman and lady from Trinidad were the occupants. An addition of four full grown men to the accommodations at hand might look to the proprietor of an eastern mansion like crowding the mourners. But Dawson said he had lived in the country 14 years and had never yet turned the first person from his doors on account of no accommodation. "You see the situation, gentlemen, and such as it is you are welcome to it." After a short call we got up to go but were prevented by Dawson who commenced to unharness the team. It was supper time and all except the children packed around an extension table in a low, black kitchen, ten feet square, containing a cooking range, a dish cupboard, and a variety of cooking and hunting utensils which hung on the wall and over head. The first appearance was not inviting, but I soon learned not to rely upon appearances. No King ever sat down to better specimens of the culinary art. Steak as tender as spring chicken, biscuits as light as a feather, and bread, graham and white, that was entitled to a first premium at the fair, sauce, preserves, pickles, etc., flavored to suit the most fastidious palate.

After supper we all packed into a room, about 12'x14' with a fire place at one end, crib in one corner, bed in another, secretary in the third, while a wash stand and half a dozen chairs completed the outfit. It was soon discovered that there was music in the company, and a place was cleared away in the center of the room, a Wood's organ brought from the entry, and the school marm, the Trinidad lady and the subscriber formed a trio for the execution of gospel hymns which drew forth rounds of applause from the crowded house.

An experience meeting followed in which Mr. Dawson related numerous hair breadth escapes from wild beasts during his 14 years of border life in New Mexico and prior to coming here. Having spent the first thirty years of his life with the cattle, wild game, and Indians of northwestern Texas, he was well prepared for the business and sports of this territory. He is a famous hunter and his home is never out of sight of big game. This season he has killed in this very neighborhood three cinnamon bears, two mountain lions, several deer, antelopes, etc. and has been on a hunt but twice. We intended to invite him to accompany us a day or two in the woods, but his building enterprise prevented.

Mr. Dawson's home place contains about 1,500 acres of excellent land and, contrary to the general rule, he does a little at farming, has a variety of fruit trees, a garden, and plants some corn. Farming was common here prior to the coming of the (Santa Fe) railroad two years ago as everyone then had either to raise his supplies or pay for hauling 700 miles from Kansas City. But it is different now. The wheat and corn fields have gone to weeds. The untold profits in stock raising and the ease with which the work is done, make the profits of the most successful farming appear like small compensation for the labor performed. Hence large land holders prefer to buy their supplies rather than be troubled with tilling the soil. Dairying and variety farming would pay better here than in Vermont, but they don't pay enough comparatively to attract much attention.

Mr. Dawson keeps on the home place a few hundred cattle, growing up in the name of his children, about 75 horses, a lot of poultry, and a pack of nine hounds, which guard the premises and are always ready to pursue the bear, the mountain lion and the deer whenever the owner inclines to indulge in a few days of sport. Dawson is an excellent specimen of the pioneer, open-hearted, cordial in his welcomes, fond of company and storytelling. He has roughed it, pinched his way along up to the present time but now counts his land by the townships and his cattle and sheep by the thousand.

Notwithstanding our packed accommodations, I awoke Wednesday morning refreshed by a good sleep. On our return we took a northern route and rode 15 miles extra through the parks and canyons of the pasture. It was an utmost charming ride and passed scenery which I never saw surpassed from the Rocky Mountain range. We passed bunch after bunch of cattle grazing in the pasture. They were not scrubs by any means but well graded up with the best Durham bulls. In this herd of 2,500 cattle, the three year old steers will average to dress 700 pounds and the twos 575. Our Vermont stockmen from these figures can form their own estimate of the quality of the herd. They have our word for it that the average Vermont stock, stall fed, will not surpass the immense New Mexican herds. It costs money to raise an ox in Vermont, but here he will grow up into fatness and money value in spite of the owner's neglect. He will take care of himself, and all the owner has to do is to keep his private mark on him and keep track of his whereabouts.

Regarding cattle, your course should be as follows: buy a straight bunch, that is, a herd of different ages. By so doing, you begin to receive income at the end of the first year. If you intend to continue a long time in the business, it will be better to buy your land. This can be done by buying water frontage for such sized herd as you desire, and the range will not cost to exceed 50 cents an acre for the amount which the watering will control. If you want to start with 2,000 head, you will aim to control 20,000 acres of land which will cost, say $10,000. Fence the range with wire, which will cost about $2,000 more, making $12,000 invested in range. In purchasing a straight herd of 2,000 head, buy cows, yearlings and two-year-old steers. The proportion will be about as follows: 1,000 cows and two-year-old heifers, 650 yearling steers and heifers and 350 two-year-old steers. Such a herd will cost from $14 to $16 per head on an average. Call it $15 for the purpose of estimate, and your herd stands you $30,000. To this add the $12,000 for the ranch, and the capital invested is $42,000. We will say you have made your purchase in July when some of the cows have calves and others are coming in. But at this season the cow and calf are reckoned as one, whether the calf is born or unborn.

You are about ready to begin. But first, buy eight horses for use on the ranch at a cost of about $400. Now brand your cattle, which will cost $100, and turn the herd onto the range. One man will be the regular force. He will have a ranch, a mud house somewhere in the pasture and will be required to ride past every rod of the wire fence daily to repair breaks and recapture cattle, if any have escaped. This service will require four horses for he will ride rapidly and change every day. The other four horses will be kept for extra help. Cowmen here make little account of horses as their keeping is inexpensive, being kept on the range near headquarters. Extra help on a cow ranch is considered equal to one-fourth of one man's time.

Sometime in August the cattle are rounded up by four riders, a few hundred at a time, and the mother cows and calves are cut out—separated from the herd—corralled and the large calves are branded, that is, the owner's peculiar mark is burned into the hide. Then they are turned loose again with the herd. This process occupies about four days.

In November the same process is repeated, and the small calves omitted in August are branded. Your mark is now on the entire herd. No extra work is required until December when the beef buyers appear. The herd is then rounded up by a force of say eight men who will ride two days and round up the whole pasture, get all the cattle into one bunch, and cut out the beef cattle for sale.

Now for the profits. The number of beeves sold out of a herd of 2,000 head would be about 350 and would consist of all the three and the best of the two-year-old steers. They will bring in ordinary seasons an average of $25 a piece or a total of $8,750 the expense for the year will be $450 for the regular man at $30 a month, and an occasional helper, $125 for board, $40 for interest on the $400 for the eight horses, and $100 for horse feed and incidentals. This estimate is liberal. Total expenses $715. Deduct this from the receipts of $8,750 leaves $8,035 or a trifle over 19 per cent interest as net profit on the capital invested. Not so very remarkable, after all, you say. But the story is not yet all told. Compare the size of your herd at the beginning with the size at the end of the year. The estimate is that 1,000 cows will produce 80 per cent of that number of calves. In order to be on the safe side, make it 75 per cent, which gives you 750 calves to be added, making the herd at the end of the year 2,750 in number. From that number deduct the 350 beeves sold out leaving 2,400 at the beginning of the second year. At $15 a head, your herd of 2,000 was worth $30,000, at the same estimate your herd of 2,400 is worth $36,000. Add this $6,000 increased value of the herd to the $8,035 net receipts gives $14,035 as the real profit of the first year, or a fraction less than 34 per cent interest on the money invested.

This estimate is made on the basis that the herder has purchased his land, the purchase money being reckoned in with the cost of the herd and so far swelling the capital invested. In free (open range) herding, which in times past has been most common, no capital was invested in land, and the profit was consequently larger. This, too, is the profit of the first year. The second year will give equal per cent on the increased value of the herd, the third the same. It is like compound interest, every year the increase goes on drawing interest. On a five year estimate the profit will amount to more than an average of 60 per cent a year on the original investment.

The general estimate of the country is that cattle raising pays a profit, over and above all expenses of 50 per cent per annum, and that no investment can be more sure to meet expectation. I know of one case where a large investment was made in cattle a year ago, and the same cattle, with increase, growth, and rise in the market, could now be sold at a net profit of nearly 100 per cent. But this is owing to fortunate buying, extra grazing and a rise in the market. It is an exception to the general rule.

A year ago last February H.M. Porter, the merchant, bought a herd of 600 cows with calves, coming yearlings, by their side, paying $16.50 for each cow with its calf. In the same purchase he got 350 steers, coming two years old, at $9 a head, making the entire herd cost $12,900. The following January he sold the 350 nine dollar steers for $16.50 each, getting a total of $5,775. During the year the cows brought another crop of calves, 480 in number, which at six months old, were sold for veal to Denver parties at a season when veal is high. They brought $9 a head, or a total of $4,320. The total sale of steers and calves amounted to $10,095. On delivery of the animals sold he failed to find 48 of the number, which were lost, strayed or stolen, for which was deducted $624, leaving amount of receipts for the sale of steers and calves at $9,471. After this sale he had on hand the cows and calves, coming two yearlings at time of purchase and now coming two years old. Allowing that five per cent of them were lost, he had 570 cows worth $13 a piece and 570 coming two-year old worth $10.50 apiece. At the time the steers and calves were sold, the remainder of the herd was therefore worth $12,395. Add to this the money obtained for the 350 steers and the veal calves sold gives the total value of receipts of the herd at $21,866, to which amount the $12,900 had grown in eleven months. Mr. Porter owned his ranch and employed two men during the time having considerable extra work to do about the ranch in fencing, repairing, etc. This extra work, interest on $400 for the eight horses, board and incidentals, all amounted to $926. Deduct this from gross value of receipts and herd, $21,866, leaves $8,040 as the net profit for the eleven months which is at the rate of 68 per cent a year.

The above figures show the opportunities for profitable investment in stock raising in New Mexico. I have taken much pains in the inquiry. The estimate given in the figures in the Porter case is below the facts, as I took the lowest figures given in receipts and the highest in expenses.

I have inquired if anyone fails in the stock raising business and am told that the instance is not known here of a man who embarks in the business, follows it legitimately, avoiding risky speculation, and fails to reap a handsome profit. The Hall brothers, after fifteen years of operation beginning with about $10,000 have just sold out their herd and ranch for $400,000 and gone to Kansas City to invest in real estate and enjoy their ease. J.E Temple commenced in 1869 with seven cows, sold milk, made butter, and grew his herd. He now owns an extra ranch and about 1,500 cattle and can sell out for $50,000. Morrisey & McChristian began eight years ago in a small way and now have about 2,000 head and a good ranch and are estimated at $50,000. Old Mr. Dawson and son started 14 years ago with 13 cows and now have 1,300 head and are worth $25,000 at least. Mr. Sculley, an Irishman, started with nothing eight years ago and now has a ranch and 700 head of cattle and is worth about $16,000. This is not in the line of Jay Gould profits, to be sure, but it must be remembered that we are speaking of a line of industry to be compared with eastern farming and not with eastern stock gambling, trading, manufacturing, or other middle business. The stock raiser is a producer, and his profits come out of the earth.

The advantage in New Mexico is that both sheep and cattle are raised without feeding and are not liable to starve to death or freeze up in the winter. Above the divide in Colorado and Kansas, feeding is seldom resorted to, but the winters are occasionally so severe that herds suffer and die. This is the advantage claimed by New Mexico operators. Colorado and Kansas operators claim profit from the business, the same as that given in the estimate for New Mexico. With favorable winters their claim in realized, but in a series of years they will fall behind New Mexico by reason of the occasional severe winter.

Agnes Morley Cleaveland's grey horse and sidesaddle. (New Mexico State University Library, Archives and Special Collections)

AGNES MORLEY CLEAVELAND

Agnes Morley Cleaveland was born in Cimarron, New Mexico Territory in 1874 where her father, William Morley, managed the sprawling Maxwell Land Grant. Later, after her father was mysteriously killed in 1883 while supervising the construction of a railroad in Mexico, her mother bought a ranch outside of Datil in the western part of the Territory and moved her family there. Agnes grew up there helping her brother Raymond on the ranch until she left for college at Stanford University in California.

In 1941 she published a collection of her experiences growing up on the Datil Ranch titled, *No Life for a Lady*. Range historian J. Frank Dobie wrote that it was "not only the best book about frontier life on the range ever written by a woman, but one of the best books concerning rangelands and range people written by anybody." Cleaveland later wrote a popular history of her hometown of Cimarron that was published under the title of *Satan's Paradise* in 1952.

In the story included here she relates an example of some of the challenges she endured being a woman in the male dominated New Mexico ranch world.

No Life for a Lady
Cambridge: The Riverside Press, 1941
Lincoln: University of Nebraska Press, 1977

"Cowpuncher on a Sidesaddle"

My brief experience as a schoolteacher over, I went back to 'making a hand.' Although I rode sidesaddle like a lady, the double standard did not exist on the ranch up to the point of my actual physical limitations, I worked side by side with the men, receiving the same praise or same censure for like undertakings. I can still hear Bowlegs scoffing at me because a 'longear' got away from me in the brush. What kind of brush rider was I that I couldn't keep close enough to a yearling to see which way it went?

Just to show what my failure consisted of, I may say that riding through the brush, or, as we called it, 'breaking brush,' is a specialized kind of cowpuncher horsemanship, just as 'hopping prairie dog holes' is another. New Mexico cowboys hooted derisively at cowboys from the plains of Texas who hesitated to ride full tilt at a clump of trees whose branches interlaced to form a veritable hedge. Texas-bred horses had the same inhibitions. On the other hand, our cowhands who had been over to the Staked Plains came back with tales of how their hair had turned white at the way Texas 'peelers' ran over prairie dog towns where there seemed to be no solid ground between the dog holes. Both seem incredibly dangerous.

'Brush-breaking' derives its name from the peculiar brittleness of the timber in the high dry altitude of the Southwest. One can ride at full speed into a piñon tree and the chances are that the momentum will develop force enough to smack off even good sized branches. 'If you can't dodge 'em, stick your chest out and break 'em,' is the rule for brush riding. And sometimes when your chest is stuck out, your horse is leaping a fallen log and doing it with a twisting motion to escape crashing headlong into the trunk of another tree which had not been visible.

I have, in my presumably saner years, ridden slowly through country where I remembered having torn at top speed in pursuit of some cow critter who had the advantage of less height than that of my horse and me combined, and have told myself that nobody ever did run a horse through that labyrinth of dead and living brush.

Some credit is, of course, due to the rider's fearlessness and skill, but more should go to the horse. Cowponies, like human beings, become specialists. There were brush horses, cutting horses, roping horses, and show-off horses. Whenever possible, every cowpuncher had one show-off horse, a high-stepper, which he rode up and down the road,' meaning wherever there might be an audience. Especially a feminine audience. 'Watch Shorty spur that old stick he's on in the off shoulder, 'cause there's a lady present,' was whispered to me more than once by some envious cowboy who was not at the moment engaged in showing off himself. Possibly we ladies showed off a bit too.

Most of our real work was done in silence. Tenderfeet always complained, with justification: 'Nobody tells me anything. How am I to know what to do?' Kibitzing was our greatest social sin. A stranger could be with a cow outfit for days without knowing who was boss. Nobody shouted orders around a cow outfit. The boss merely picked up his bridle and started for the corral. Sometime during the process of saddling he managed to convey to the other riders that the drive would take in such and such territory and that so and so could work the Rincon or west pass Piñon flat. And the man rode off in silence, each knowing what to do and needing all his resources to do it.

'Chasing cattle' was a phrase the uninitiated often used. Well, we 'chased' them as little as possible. The object was, of course, to see that they went where we wanted them to go, and often this entailed racing with them until the horseman got in the lead and could turn them back. But chasing is hardly the word. We were given to saying disgustedly, 'That tenderfoot "chased" the steer clear out of the country; seemed to think he had his horse down to a run, but he was never out of a high lope.'

Strange how often newcomers thought their horse was running when he wasn't. The horse knew it, too, and didn't put on that extra ounce of steam which distinguishes a running horse from a galloping one.

The classic *faux pas* of all was for two tenderfeet to take after the same animal and 'make a lane,' which is to say, to get one on either side of the quarry and ride just fast enough to keep it between them.

On such occasions someone would be sure to bellow: 'That's right! Make a lane!' and then dash out and really head off the animal.

I never made lanes, and I knew when to keep out of the way. In fact, after fifty years, I vaingloriously affirm that I enjoyed a local reputation in the one field where reputations most counted—that of good horsemanship. To prove it, I cherished for years a clipping from *Mine and Lariat*, an early weekly paper which flourished briskly but briefly in Magdalena. It informed our local reading public that 'Miss Agnes of the Datils and Three-Fingered Pete are the best riders in the country.'

Even though I didn't rope and brand and do the harder and harsher part of the cow business, there was usually some place where I could function profitably. The time I 'represented' when Bud Jones came through with his trail herd was more or less typical of the sort of duty I might be called upon to perform.

When large herds passed through the country, it was impossible, of course, to avoid 'picking up' cattle of other owners across whose range the herd was traveling. So, it was customary to allow such self-invited visitors to remain until the entire herd had reached the last confines of their owner's presumed range, and then ask the owner himself to ride through, inspect every brand, and cut the herd. This was a courtesy never to be omitted.

When a big herd was to be cut, owners or their representatives often numbered a score or more. 'Working the herd' was the pinnacle of cow work. It was here that a degree of expertness came into play that never ceased to amaze me, accustomed as I was to it. Only men and horses who were masters of their craft were permitted in a herd. The man must recognize the brands, earmarks, and flesh marks instantly and unerringly, and the horse, once the cow to be taken out was indicated, must work his quarry to the edge of the herd, then 'push' it out, the rider assisting only at this critical moment by a yell or slap of his quirt or bridle reins upon leather chaps.

Another rider is waiting to 'push' the animal on into a smaller group of 'cuts' or culls, which are being held at some little distance away. It requires the best horsemanship to prevent the first few cattle in the smaller herd, called the 'cut,' from rushing back into the fancied protection of the larger group, so that to be assigned to 'hold the cut' is to be awarded one's cowpunching diploma.

On the day Bud Jones brought his herd across our range, Ray was unable to inspect it in the interests of our outfit and I was sent to 'represent.' I reported to Mr. Jones. By his side, on a wiry cowpony with a knowing eye, sat his ten-year-old son Jimmy, an exact replica of his father in every detail of accouterment—boots, chaps, spurs, sombrero— all cut to size. The other cowboys, perhaps twelve to fifteen, gathered around, less to receive their orders than to hear Jimmy and me receive ours.

'W-a-ll,' drawled Bud Jones, a twinkle in his eye, 'I reckon we'll let Jimmy here and Miss Agnes hold the cut right over by that patch of timber.'

The twinkle passed from eye to eye among the cowboys. 'Over by that patch of timber' was no place to hold a cut, and a girl on a sidesaddle and a ten-year-old boy the least reasonable of all possible choices for attempting it.

Should I refuse and stand forever discredited for having violated the code which allows no one to refuse an order from the boss, or submit to playing the lead in a Roman holiday for a bunch of gleeful cow waddies? Jimmy was already headed for his proper post, midway between the rim of the herd and the timber patch. I followed, inwardly raging.

The first animal to be worked out of the herd, by the elder Jones himself, was a rangy two-year-old steer. Here was gross violation of proper procedure, which called for a seasoned old cow, preferably one with a calf, as the unit which would most probably stand quietly until joined by enough others to give the bunch a feeling of solidarity.

'What the hell?' growled Jimmy, but he bent over his pony's neck and took in behind the steer. I got around between it and the timber patch just in time to keep the animal from dashing through it and on and on to liberty. Next came a long yearling. Any cowman will see instantly what was up.

One by one the cowboys drove out for us to hold the snakiest, orneriest, most fractious critters they could find—just to see us ride. Well, I couldn't see myself ride, but I could see Jimmy when I had time to look. He would lie along his pony's neck in a flank-to-flank race with some cow brute until his horse got a nose-length ahead, then he'd lean over and slap the animal in the face with a length of rope and both would turn in their tracks with such sudden reversal of speed that it seemed incredible anything not anchored tight to the horse could stay on it. It was horsemanship of the first order.

In due course the cut grew until it was large enough to satisfy the new arrivals and everything quieted down.

Then Jimmy dashed around from his side and sat his horse back on its haunches in front of me. 'By God, girl, you ride all right,' he told me.

I was deeply flattered. Jimmy's was expert judgment. He flung a leg over his saddle horn and, thus relaxed, did me the honor of settling down for a chat. He opened up with small talk. Eyeing a large rent in my riding skirt he remarked, 'a feller needs chaps in this here brush to keep from gittin' his clos' tore off.'

I agreed, and he went on: 'But chaps won't keep you from gittin' yore face tore off. I like to lost my face a coupla times lately.' Then, the small talk disposed of, he got down to business.

'You carry a gun?' he wanted to know.

Not to lose standing in his eyes, I replied a little vaguely but truthfully, 'Oh, sometimes.'

Jimmy did not, I think, look back over his shoulder, but his manner suggested it.

'What size?'

'Thirty-two,' I told him. 'It doesn't kick so hard.'

This time he did look back. 'How about tradin' for a few thirty-two cat'r'dges?'

I looked for the first time at the row of cartridges in his belt. They were forty-fives. His pistol was a thirty-two.

I shook my head. 'I'm short on thirty-twos,' I said equivocally.

Jimmy sighed in disgust. 'Don't seem like they's any thirty-twos in the country. I been tryin' to git some, but it don't seem like anybody's got any.'

Not for a ten-year-old, we hadn't. Not even for one who made a hand in a cow outfit. His father told me later that his one nagging fear was that sooner or later Jimmy would get his thirty-twos. 'And then no tellin' what!'

I didn't suggest that Jimmy might be forbidden to wear a gun of any caliber. I knew that Father Jones would shrink from any such form of cruelty to children.

James H. Cook

James H. Cook

Born in Michigan in 1857, James Cook left for Texas at age sixteen looking for adventure. There he learned to cowboy herding Longhorn cattle in the chaparral of South Texas. In 1874 he joined a trail herd that drove steers to Abilene, Kansas where they were shipped east on the railroad. He subsequently went up the trail four more times, once going as far as the Sioux reservation in Dakota Territory.

In 1878, after his last trail drive, he stayed in Wyoming and spent the next five years guiding big game hunters in the northern Rockies. Afterward, he journeyed to southwestern New Mexico to manage the WS Ranch owned by one of his English hunters, Harold Wilson. His time on the WS coincided with a series of raids by Apaches, led by Geronimo, who had escaped from their Arizona reservation in 1885. A description of Cook's involvement with the outbreak is included here.

Cook had always loved the northern Plains country where he had trailed cattle as a young man. As a result, in 1887 he left New Mexico and established a ranch on the Niobrara River in Nebraska where he died in 1942.

Fifty Years on the Old Frontier
Norman: University of Oklahoma Press, 1957

"Geronimo"

In the fall of 1882, after a most enjoyable big game hunt in the Big Horn Mountains with a number of English gentlemen whom I had guided on previous annual hunting trips in the Rocky Mountains, I went to southwestern New Mexico with those same gentlemen. They were about to engage in cattle ranching, and I assisted them in purchasing and managing some large ranch properties in that country, making my headquarters in Keller Valley, on the San Francisco River, about eighty miles north and west of Silver City, on a ranch purchased by one of my English hunting friends, Mr. Harold C. Wilson of Cheltenham, England. I was general manager of this ranch from the time of its purchase until 1887. I used a "WS" brand on all the cattle and horses purchased or raised by Mr. Wilson, and this ranch was soon known among the cattlemen of New Mexico as the WS Ranch. My other English sportsmen friends purchased large ranch properties within a radius of fifty miles of the WS, and I assisted them whenever needed in the management of their ranches while I remained in New Mexico.

The WS Ranch was at that time some distance from a railroad, Deming being the nearest railway point. A stage ran to Silver City each day, drawn by six horses. At the time of which I write, one of Wells, Fargo & Company's most noted shotgun messengers, Dan Tucker, helped guard the passengers and treasure carried by the stages. Tucker had some thrilling experiences with stage robbers in the Southwest. He had the reputation of being one of the bravest of the many gunfighters of the southwest borderlands. Guarding treasure entrusted to the care of Wells, Fargo & Company was a pretty hazardous occupation in the bandit infested country at that time. New Mexico contained its full quota of bad men, both white and black, and redskins at times caused the ranchmen, freighters, miners, and mail carriers to go heavily armed and ready for war at any moment.

It was an interesting country to me for several reasons. Evidence of a prehistoric race of people abounded on all sides. There was also proof of prehistoric life in the shape of petrified bones of extinct animals deposited in the sedimentary rocks, and tracks of flying reptile or prehistoric birds may be seen there to this day. These ancient tracks stand up on the lava rocks like the raised type used by the blind. They were evidently made while the lava rock was still soft, the pressure of the feet having doubtless made the material firmer than the surrounding material. The undisturbed lava rock has settled more than that where the pressure was applied and left the tracks standing out plainly on the surface of the rock.

For an unknown length of time before that coming of the whites, this section of the country had been the home of the Apache tribes of Indians. The Apaches have the reputation of having been the most warlike and merciless savages with whom the people of the United States ever had to contend in their winning of the West. Some of the instances of their savagery, such as the murder and butchery of Judge McComas and his wife and the abduction and murder of their little son, Charlies, are matters of recorded history. Of the many travelers on the old southern trails to California—prospectors and others—who have been wiped out by Apaches during the territorial days of New Mexico and Arizona, but few written records have, I think, been kept.

At the time of my advent into that country, some evidence could still be obtained of a few persons, at least, who had met death at the hands of Apaches. Visible proof could be seen in the form of parts of the skeletons, or often whole skeletons, of white men, bearing the marks of bullets, knives, and arrows, skulls crushed by blows from stones, and other such evidence. Metal buttons and buckles, and even parts of clothing, stored near by the pack rats, often added their mute testimony to these deeds of bloodshed and human suffering. One unfortunate fellow, whose bones I found down in a canyon in the Mogollon Mountains, had tried to scratch a few words on the side of a cliff nearby with his knife, the rusted blade of which I discovered. The writing was so weathered away that I could not decipher it. A thigh bone badly smashed by a bullet, and a partially rusted iron arrow point lying among the bones, as if it had been imbedded in his body, told a little story of the thrilling scene which had been enacted there.

The country about the ranches which we established had been, just previously to our coming, the stronghold of the old Apache chiefs, Mangus Colorado, Cochise, and Victorio. After the killing of Victoria, a short time before our arrival, there was a lull in the Indian troubles, until the summer of 1885. Then came the Geronimo outbreak.

Up to the time of the establishment of the WS Ranch, the cattlemen of southwestern New Mexico had no roundup system of handling their herds. Every ranchman looked after his own stock, each by his own method. Soon after my arrival, I helped organize a stockman's association, with a system of roundups similar to that employed on the northern cattle ranges. I superintended the western division of these roundups for the first two years of their existence in Socorro and Grant Counties. This work on the range made me familiar with the country lying between the Mogollon Range of mountains and the Arizona and Old Mexico boundary lines. This knowledge proved valuable to me, and perhaps to others, when one of the worst Indian campaigns in the Southwest came on.

Two of my friends had purchased a ranch near the San Francisco River about thirty miles north of my headquarters and named it the SU Ranch. An English friend of theirs had been visiting with them during the summer of 1885 and on numerous occasions this gentleman had ridden down to visit with me at the WS. One day he came down to see me and also to say goodbye for he planned to start for his English home in the near future. The day before he left the WS we were out hunting quail nearly all day, little dreaming of what was to happen within the next few hours. The following morning about nine o'clock, he bade me farewell and started for the SU Ranch. About half an hour later a man riding at full speed dashed up to the ranch house and shouted that Indians had been chasing him. Judging from the number he had seen, he thought all the Indians at San Carlos and Camp Apache must have broken off their reservations. He was so frightened and excited that he could scarcely talk, but at last made out to inform me that he and some companions had camped near Blue Creek, about ten miles west of the WS Ranch that morning and that a large party of Indians had attacked their camp and killed his companions. He was bringing in the saddle and pack horses to camp when the Indians jumped them and being mounted he had escaped. I told him ride to Alma, a little mining settlement about a mile and a half distant and warn the people living there.

My brother and all the cowboys employed at the ranch were that day branding calves out on the range. Charlie Moore, an old employee whose duty was to look after the bands of saddle and stock horses on the range was the only person at the men's house. A housekeeper and a Mexican boy about sixteen years of age, with myself, were all then living at the main ranch house. As soon as the rider who had brought the warning had started for Alma, I hurried into the house and notified the housekeeper and the boy. We went to the storeroom and got a lot of empty gunny sacks. Hastily filling them with sand from the garden, we piled them in the deep windows of the adobe house, leaving only loopholes from which to fire. We then opened several cases of cartridges and placed them near the arms they fitted. We always kept a good supply of arms and ammunition at the ranch. Charlie Moore soon came in. When he heard the Indian news, he said that he had been out toward Blue Creek that morning but had seen no Indian sign, and it was his verdict that the bearer of the news must have been either drunk or crazy. I told him that we would go out and get in as many of the saddle horses as possible, anyway, and guard them until we knew the truth.

We rode out at once and brought in as many of the saddle animals as we could get handily into a corral near the bunkhouse. Soon after we had started out, a party of five men from Alma came to the ranch after me. They wanted me to go with them out on the range to ascertain if any Indians were in the neighborhood. Not finding me, they had started on as the people in the Alma and Cooney mining camps were greatly alarmed by the fresh tidings of an Apache outbreak, both of these places having been besieged by Apaches before. This party of men, when but a few miles from the ranch, was fired upon by a party of Indians lying in ambush and two of them instantly killed. The names of the murdered men were Calvin Orwig and Nat Luse. The rest of the party escaped by running back through the brush and rocks.

Just as Charlie Moore and I corralled the saddle horses, an animal which had been ridden by one of the party from Alma came running to the corral with the bridle and saddle on. When we caught him, we saw that both horse and saddle covered with blood. We well knew enough then that someone had been shot, and we made up our minds that Indians were in the country.

I had two teams of driving horses in a small pasture near the house, and I sent Moore to get them. I rode up on a little hill near the house, where I could see the animals in the pasture and, also, get a shot at anyone who attempted to prevent Moore from securing them. He had ridden but a short distance into the pasture when I saw a string of Indians, about twenty-five in number, part mounted and the rest on foot, moving directly toward the horses. Moore, who could not see the Indians, was riding directly toward them. I tried to stop him by shouting, but he apparently did not hear me, and I immediately opened fire on the Indians with a 40-90 Sharps rifle at a range of about one thousand yards. This checked them, and they ran to cover in the rocks and brush. The horses in the pasture, when the Indians returned my fire, stampeded and came running to their stable. Moore located the Indians by their firing and, getting onto high ground where he could see them, helped me send a few leaden compliments to speed the parting guests. They made a good run back into the mountains. In doing so, they had to cross some fairly open ground, but the range, with such rapidly moving targets, was too great for us. I could not see that our bullets injured any of them.

Night was coming on, and Charlie and I returned to the house. We stood guard all night, he at the corrals and I at the main ranch house. I took my pistols and two double-barreled shotguns loaded with buckshot and stayed outside within the shadow of the buildings, there being some moonlight. Just as day was breaking, the housekeeper called me to come in and get some coffee. At the time I was standing by the side of an adobe storehouse about fifteen feet from the kitchen door. I went in, drank a cup of coffee and returned to my station. To my surprise I observed the tracks of two Indians within a few feet of the spot. One savage had worn moccasins, the other had bare feet. I was certainly startled, but I soon saw, by their tracks in the soft earth of the garden, that they had left the place. I signaled Charlie to come to me, and when he arrived, we followed the tracks a short distance. We concluded that, as the Indians were trying to conceal their tracks, we might be able to overtake and get a shot of them.

It was now daylight, and we followed the trail of these Indians to the top of a hill a short distance from the ranch. At this point we discovered that they had been joined by several other Indians. With my field glasses I took a look over the trails that led into the Mogollon Mountains. Looking over on what was called the Deep Creek trail, I could see a line of objects moving along. They were too far away to be seen plainly, but as no range stock had ever traveled over the trail, I was sure the objects were Indians.

We returned to the ranch. After getting some breakfast, Charlie and I rode out to the top of a high hill about a mile west of the ranch, where we could look over our horse range. Leaving our animals hidden in a clump of cedar trees, we climbed to a place in the rocks where we could get a good view of the surrounding country with our powerful field glasses. I soon detected some objects moving along on the Eagle Creek trail. This trail led within a hundred yards of the point where we were hidden. The moving objects were coming toward us, and as they came nearer, I could make out about a dozen Indians on foot and a white man mounted on a mule following them. He wore a suit of brown overalls. The ground along the trail at the place where it passed us was quite free of brush and rocks.

Charlie said, "Let's let them come right up close to us and kill the whole outfit before they can get to cover."

I told him to wait until I started shooting. By this time they were within a hundred yards of us. Letting them come still closer, I called out, "Halt! Don't try to run!"

The man on the mule pulled up instantly, and the Indians after a word from him, stood still.

"Who are you?" I demanded.

"I'm Lieutenant Gatewood, and these men are Indian scouts," he replied.

I thereupon rose up in plain view and told the Lieutenant to come nearer, but to let the Indians stay where they were. He did so, approaching to within thirty yards of us. He then asked who I was. When I told him my name, he asked if I were Jim Cook, the hunter and guide of whom he had so often heard Captain Emmett Crawford speak. I told him that I probably was as Captain Crawford was one of my friends.

Gatewood then told me that he had been stationed at Camp Apache in command of a company of Indian scouts; that Geronimo and his band had broken away from their reservation where they had been held prisoners, and that he had got together a few of his men and started in pursuit. He said he was being closely followed by a pack train and two troops of the Fourth U.S. Cavalry commanded by Captain Allen Smith and Lieutenant Parker. Looking back along the Eagle Creek trail, I could see the troops coming. Gatewood had left the trail of the Indians a short distance back, and he and the troops were rushing for the nearest point on the San Francisco River to give the command a chance to get food and water. They had traveled about seventy miles over very rough mountain trails, hardly stopping for food or rest, and both men and horses were very tired. Many of their animals had lost their shoes and traveling over the hard volcanic rocks had so worn their hoofs that they limped painfully. I told Gatewood where I thought he could strike the main trail of the Indians over at Deep Creek thus making a big cutoff.

While the troops were getting breakfast, a man from Alma arrived and told me that the Indians had killed two of the men who had gone out the day before with the scouting party. He wanted to know if I would go and help find the bodies and bring them in. He told me the direction which the party had taken and, as it was near where the troops would travel if they went to Deep Creek to strike the Indians trail, I asked Captain Smith if he would help me search for the bodies. He replied that he would, and we soon started. We located the bodies without any trouble. They were lying within a few feet of the trail in which they had been traveling.

I then accompanied the troops to the place on the Deep Creek trail where I had observed the moving objects. It proved to be the trail which had been followed by the main body of Indians. I turned back from this point, went to the ranch, got some men from Alma and went out and packed the bodies of Orwig and Luse on two horses and the men from Alma took them home for burial.

Charlie Moore and I then rode to Devil's Park, a spot in the mountains so named by gold prospectors because of its hidden situation. The main trail of the Indians led in that direction. A man named Stallworth and his family were living there in a little log cabin home. We wanted to ascertain whether the Indians had molested them. When, from a point near where the cabin was located, we heard some rapid firing, we knew that an attack on the Stallworth's was being made. Leaving our horses concealed in a thicket, we hurried to the aid of our neighbors and friends. Two of Geronimo's warriors ceased shooing into that cabin very suddenly when we opened fire upon them. The rest of the attacking band, twelve or fifteen in number, made a hasty departure to the rough shelter of timber and gulches close at hand, firing a few shots back at us as they ran. Doubtless they did not know the number in the party which had come to the rescue or the incident might have ended differently. I believe that the two Indians who did not run away when their companions started so hurriedly into the Mogollon Mountains were the first to lose their lives at the hands of white men after starting on their murderous trip from Camp Apache. Whether our bullets injured any of the others we never knew for we did not follow them. The Apaches at that time were, as a rule, very poor shots with firearms. Most of the white persons killed by them were fired upon short range from cover. In the art of concealment and ambuscade they were as expert, I think, as any savages on the American continent.

When the firing was over, I called to Mr. Stallworth, and he came out of the cabin with his family. Mrs. Stallworth had been wounded, and we first cared for her, after which we listened to their story. Just a short time before out arrival, Mrs. Stallworth had been out upon the doorstep of the cabin, giving the children their morning lessons. Looking up from her work, she had seen an Indian with a gun stealthily making his way from behind one tree to another within a short distance of the house. She instantly grabbed her children and hurried them into the house. Just as she closed and barred the door, a bullet crashed through the planks and tore its way through her arm. Mr. Stallworth was in the house repairing a saddle when the attack started. He had a rifle and was a good shot but had allowed his supply of ammunition to run low and had but two or three cartridges upon which he could depend. These he did not want to use until forced to. He told me that he had taken one cartridge which had missed fired and tried it from a loophole on an Indian at a very short range, but it failed to explode.

Mrs. Stallworth, in giving her version of the attack, said, "I kept telling Stallworth to shoot, but he refused to shoot for quite a while. At last, he pulled the trigger, but the gun merely snapped. We have plenty of cartridges but no ammunition." She meant by this that they had plenty of empty cartridge shells but not powder and ball for them.

Sending Charlie Moore to Alma to get people to move this family to a place of safety, I remained with the Stallworths until help arrived. We felt that a second attack by the Indians might be made at any moment. As it was seldom that the bodies of Indians slain in battle were left without an effort by their brother warriors to secure them, we expected that a move of this sort might be made. However, when Mr. Stallworth returned to his home several days later, after taking his family to Alma, he discovered that his hogs and the coyotes and buzzards had left but little for him to dispose of by way of Indian remains.

John H. (Jack) Culley

Jack Culley was born in England in 1864 and came to New Mexico to visit friends at age twenty-four after graduation from the University of Oxford. He liked the ranch life he experienced and decided to stay and try his hand at cowboying. For the next several years he worked on a number of outfits around Wagon Mound and in 1893 was hired as range manager of the sprawling Bell Ranch that straddled the Canadian River on the eastern side of the Territory.

After riding for the Bells for five years, he returned to the Wagon Mound country and went into the cattle business for himself establishing the Rafter C Bar Ranch. He sold the ranch and cattle in 1916 at age fifty-two and then joined the United States Army serving throughout World War I. He had become an American citizen in 1900.

After the war he returned to his native England but eventually came back to the United States and settled in Los Angeles. Among other activities, he began writing about his time in the saddle on the New Mexico range. Most of his stories were published in the *Western Livestock Journal* headquartered in Denver. They are marked by their fidelity to the range rider's work and speech.

In the late 1930s he collected some of his favorite stories from the *Journal* and published them under the title *Cattle, Horses, and Men of the Western Range* in 1940. In the excerpts included here he relates the tragic stories of two animal outlaws who roamed the Bell Ranch range, one a mare called La Vaqueta and the other an enormous spotted Longhorn bull. In addition, he sings the praises of one of his favorite horses that he called Silver.

John H. (Jack) Culley

Cattle, Horses, and Men of the Western Ranges
Los Angeles: The Ward Ritchie Press, 1940
Tucson: University of Arizona Press, 1985

"Outlaws of the Range"

I've told you how rich in grazing land the Bell pasture is. The rim rocks are about the only part that doesn't grow feed. For all that, there is plenty of as wild country as I ever rode over. It is mostly around the edges. I remember when I first went down there, I thought I'd take a look at the main grant fence. To my surprise, that job occupied me just two weeks. I never took so long, before or since, to ride one hundred and twenty-eight miles. And then I'd sometimes be afoot, or just taking a bird's-eye view of the fence from the rim rock of a canyon. Every old fence rider will recall the little labor-saving dodges, like that, we used in "ridin' fence!"

Well, wild country, such as that is, makes wild cattle and horses; and some of them become outlaws, as we used to call them. It's about that kind of outlaws I thought I'd tell you now.

The tendency to resist restraint seems to be strong in every normal living thing—human or of the animal order. You will notice it in the little tot in your own family the minute he begins to toddle. He indicates a determined desire to escape. In the same way you'll find the average bunch of rested horses reluctant to enter a corral, and they'll make wild whoopee as soon as they are turned out of it. Whenever, in consequence of rough country and the advantages it gives an animal to get away, or through bad handling or any other cause, a horse succeeds for a number of times in dodging the corral gate and effectually escaping his pursuers, there becomes established in him what we may call the "habit of escape." Thereafter, actually, he would sooner break his neck than

71

submit to being driven or corralled. In short—if you happen to be the owner of him—you've got an outlaw on your hands.

At best, corralling broncos was not a light job. You had to have a horse with a right good turn of speed, and long-winded. There must be plenty of the good readers of these pages who have run broncos in the old range days. It won't be necessary for me to tell them what a fellow's inner feelings are when, after chasing a band of mares for half a day, it suddenly stops and scatters on him just as he gets it to the corral gate. You'll agree with me, I believe, that at that moment life touched the bottom. And you'll sympathize with my old friend, George Crocker.

George was out one day after a bunch of bronco mares. He aimed to corral them at the stockyard on the Santa Fe railroad which runs through that part of the country. They had been giving him and his boys some considerable helluva time, but at last they had them straightened out for the corral gate and almost within the wing. It so happened that at that moment a freight train was coming along, and just when the engine got opposite the corral gate, the engineer, thinking to have a little fun, gave three sharp toots with his whistle. That was enough; the broncos stopped short in their tracks, wheeled, broke—and away to the tules!

George is one of the quietest men I ever knew, but he got down off his horse, unlimbered his .44 carbine, and sent three bullets in quick succession through the engineer's cab. Fortunately—or unfortunately, according as you view the matter—the engineer was not hit. He lived to run other trains, I suppose, but not, one believes, to try out practical jokes on range men corralling broncos.

When I first went down to the Bells, there were about twelve hundred broncos scattered all over the large range. This was unsatisfactory for many reasons. The bunches were hard to find when we wanted to brand colts in the fall or to break them in the spring. Then, gentle saddle horses would get out of the horse pastures and go off with them. So, we decided to gather up everything and locate the whole lot on the Mesa Rica, a large mesa fenced on two sides by the south and west grant fence, and on the remaining sides by rim rocks.

There was a well-known brown mare running on the range at that time. She had been roped years before, but had broken the rope and got away, and from that day to the time I'm writing of, no one had ever been able to corral her. The rope they had caught her with had been a rawhide one and it broke right at her throat, and the noose stuck there around her neck and had been there ever since. So the Mexicans called her La Vaqueta, which is Spanish for the 'the strap;' and by that name the brown Bell mare was known the length and breadth of that country. My last words to Tom Kane, the wagon boss, when he started on the hunt, were, "Be sure and get La Vaqueta." "Never fear," said Tom.

As soon as the boys got the general range worked and the mares gathered and on the mesa, I rode over to see the thing finished up. I found them driving somewhere between one thousand and twelve hundred head. The ground was broken, and I thought the herd, with La Vaqueta, fat as butter, in the lead of it, inclined to be restive, so, taking an opportunity, I slipped in at the head of them. It's not usual to drive horses from the point like that, and when Tom Kane saw me there, he hollered to me he was afraid I'd break up the herd. I hollered back, "Look here, Tom Kane, you leave this job to me. I'll lead this here bunch of broncs into the ranch post office, if you say you want them there."

Of course, it's a ticklish job riding right bang in front of a bunch like that. It's like handling a six-shooter with a hair trigger. Yet, as a matter of fact, the wilder the individual animals in a herd, the more sensitive to the point, and, therefore, the easier to control. What you need is a quick pair of eyes and a good horse—alert, yet perfectly steady. Anyhow, I never remember in all my range experience enjoying anything more than pointing that herd of broncs. It isn't every day you get a chance at over a thousand of them, all wild, in one lot. To see the whole herd swing, and sway, and swerve this way or that, as easy as water flowing—in response to the slightest movement on my part—was a beautiful and exciting experience.

At length the fellows on circle had all the pockets worked, and we started down the long draw leading to the corrals. Once inside, Tom wanted to catch La Vaqueta, to take off the strap and see how she acted. So, we ran her off with a few others into a catching pen, and someone caught her by the neck, and we lined up on the rope to choke her down. But it wasn't necessary. She never stirred. The brown mare lay there as dead as a doornail. Too bad, La Vaqueta! We had broken your heart.

I have just told you how we corralled the brown outlaw mare, La Vaqueta. How we roped her and threw her, and how we broke her heart. Too bad, indeed, I remember thinking; and I don't believe there was one of the boys of the outfit but felt a pang of sympathy for the brave old mare that died sooner than surrender. May we all be a stout-spirited as that!

But, as every cowman knows, cattle on a rough range get every bit as wild as horses. The roughest country we had on the Bell Ranch was the brakes of the Atarque. It isn't rough in the sense that much of Arizona is; it's on an altogether smaller scale, and not really mountain at all. But it's as rough as a country can be, and yet be good grazing. It might, perhaps, be best described as a wild scatter of parks and pockets, cut up in every possible direction by steep and rocky ridges, over which narrow trails lead from park to park. The boys on circle were always cautioned to work carefully and make as little noise as possible. You might sight a bunch of cattle in an open park and slip around it; but let them once get wind of you and they would hit it for the nearest trail and be gone like a flash. And with the best rock horse in the world you'd be lucky to get sight of them again that day, much less catch them.

I suppose we could have got a lot of these outlaws out by making a special work, or by contract. Up on the Mesa the Wagon Mound and Watrous cattle associations, which represented the range cattlemen of those districts, paid ten dollars for every outlaw animal brought out of the Mora and Red River breaks. I remember planning, one time, with my brother-in-law, Harry McKellar, to take over a contract. Harry was a crack hand, and I thought I had the best horse for roping in rocks in New Mexico. (And I'm still not sure I hadn't.) But the Bells during my time never made any special effort; just depended on the regular outfit to get out whatever it could.

Under such conditions there were "critters" that got away every year and finally became outlaws. Cows and steers were running in those breaks, as old as 15 or 20 years, that had never been in a roundup since they were branded. One old spotted steer all the old Bell hands knew. A perfect specimen of Texas Longhorn he was, tall and gaunt and narrow, with a tremendous spread of horns, and warier and speedier than a deer.

One day on the fall roundup two of the boys came upon this old chap and succeeded in cutting him off. Riding good horses, they ran onto him and laid their lines (ropes) on him, brought him in to camp and joined him with the day herd. A day or two after, he was driven down to the headquarters ranch and corralled there, with the idea of dehorning him and turning him loose in the horse pasture till we got ready to ship. The wildest cow brute will become tractable if you take off his horns.

Well, they got his horns off, opened the corral gate and turned him loose. The poor old fellow was sore and wrathy as he came out of the corral. He looked all around him for someone to take it out on. But not a soul was to be seen. The ground floor of that ranch at that particular moment was totally deserted. What population there was, was situated on the top rail of corral gates and other objects off the ground. There was a large open shed in the center of the yard and the old man went over there, moving with a queer little scuttle, and rummaged around for a while among the buggies and chuck wagons and blacksmith's outfits, etc. but there was clearly no business to be done there, as the only man in the shed had climbed on top of a chuck box, and the steer seemed on the point of quitting the premises altogether when his eye fell on a narrow gap in a brick wall that formed an enclosure around the main ranch dwelling.

I was standing inside this enclosure, tinkering with something close beside the kitchen door, the steer having passed out of my mind for the moment, when all of a sudden, lo and behold, his bovine nibs pops through the hole in the wall within a few feet of me and, tickled to find a victim at last, comes at me head down, snuffing. I did not wait to argue the point with him; I executed an immediate retirement through the kitchen door, lowering all records for events of that sort. The old fellow seemed puzzled at my sudden disappearance, but, after a moment's consideration he turned and trotted back through the wall and, finding no one outside, scuttled away along the road leading east through the pasture and disappeared in a dip of the creek.

A couple of hours or so after, about sundown, someone coming in to the ranch reported seeing an animal lying in the creek a hundred yards or so below the house. So, I went down to investigate. There, sure enough, was the old spotted steer, stretched out full length in the middle of the creek. It was dusk and the water flowing past his body gave an appearance of movement to it. But as I came up to him, I saw at once that the old steer would range the pastures no longer. When he left the kitchen door and disappeared from view in the dip of the creek, he had run into the first pool he encountered, shoved his head under the water and deliberately drowned himself.

Too bad; we had broken another old outlaw's heart.

I have explained on an earlier page (for the benefit of inexperienced readers) what really constituted an outlaw animal on the range. Certain horses or cow brutes by dint of managing a number of times to escape being corralled or caught, contracted a violent objection to having their freedom interfered with in any manner whatsoever. They'd break their own necks sooner than enter a corral. I've told you how we broke La Vaqueta's heart, the brown mare that ran so long on the Bell range, by roping and throwing her; and how the old outlaw longhorn steer out of the Atarque breaks, after we caught him and dehorned him, went off into the creek and drowned himself. And I've given you Oat Martine's story about the bunch of bronco mares the boys ran onto a rocky point in Hell Canyon, and that jumped off and killed themselves. I am inclined to think that the career of the animal outlaw, like that of the human one, usually ended in disaster.

There wasn't very many such animals, certainly. We didn't encourage them because they had the effect of spoiling other gentle stock they got with. I can't tell you how Black Jack, the AI Bar bald-faced black I have in mind, got spoiled, for the AI Bar horse herd in which he was raised was a mighty gentle one and well handled. But he was naturally a high-headed, wild eyed brute, who single-footed, and horses with natural saddle gaits usually have a touch of eccentricity about them. Anyhow Black Jack got out of the AI Bar pastures and was heard of all over the range, keeping carefully shut of anything that looked like an enclosure or saddle rope. So, I was surprised when Old Man Turner's boy, Allie, offered to sell him to me one day, saddle and bridle broke. It appeared that Allie and his cousin, Bud, had spotted the horse running on the Cerro Pelon or Bald Mountain, that lies just west of the Turkey Mountains, and had bought him on the range. There's a long fence on the Cerro Pelon and into an angle of it the boys managed to work Black Jack and get one throw at him. It wasn't long before they had him in a corral and saddled. I gave Allie twenty-five dollars for him.

He turned out a free and easy gaited saddle horse, mighty tough, and gentle enough if you gave him plenty of riding. I took him for a while as my own mount. Eventually, as I was leaving the ranch for the winter, John Hinde, ranch foreman, took him over for a winter horse on account of his easy gaits.

But John and Black Jack didn't hit it off. Now you expect a range horse to cut up a bit when he comes up fat and rested at the beginning of the summer work. But it's a different matter when one insists on staging a private rodeo show every frosty morning. One day Black Jack put on an extra scandalous performance. The bald-faced black was long in the legs and John's are short, and nothing approaching a contact was possible. In cases like this some men react in one way, some in another. I've known men content to let loose a flow of pure profanity which may or may not have impressed the horse. John is not like that. He wastes no words in emergencies. He walked back to the house, some fifty yards away, and when he returned to the corral he had with him his big .45 Colt's revolver, and he applied it to that part of Black Jack's anatomy where it puts 'em to sleep soonest. He described the whole affair to me when I got back to the ranch and remarked to him that I didn't notice Black Jack anywhere around.

I have suggested in some other place that his outlaw spirit, this dislike of restraint or confinement, is congenital in all animals, human included. Nevertheless it may well be that it is stronger in some cases than others. It's hard to believe that the instinct of escape isn't more pronounced, for instance, in the mustang than in the more domestically bred horse. I happen to have handled some pure mustangs straight off the range in Chihuahua. They broke perfectly gentle and indeed I found them particularly tractable. But one day after they were thoroughly accustomed to life on the ranch they got away from the gentle horse herd, and off by themselves on the open range. No sooner did they find themselves free that they hit it for the Ocate Mesa, a steep and rugged bluff three or four miles distant. We never had a show to stop or turn them. Once there they climbed up under the rim rock, and I have a particularly clear remembrance of those little wild creatures running along the rock mesa side, looking down at us as they ran. Deer couldn't have appeared wilder or have shown a sharper instinct of escape.

Mighty persistent was this wild blood. Some of these Chihuahua mares were bred to a half-bred Percheron, or Norman, as we called it in those days. I bought one of their colts and made a cowhorse out of him—the best I ever owned or rode. Although he never got over a strong propensity to pitch, he showed up just like an average cowhorse. I found him just as teachable as the original mares. And perhaps it wouldn't hurt if I were to break into my narrative here to give you a brief description of the little horse, for I think he was a remarkable one, and it may help my readers to kind of picture him to themselves as my story of him runs along.

Silver—he was silver white from head to heels—was what you call a big-little horse. He stood barely fourteen hands, I believe. He had the perfect conformation of the Percheron; the power and substance. But through these ran all the litheness and spring of the Arab. He was a living example of controlled energy. He could stop dead short going at top speed without giving you a suspicion of a jar. This is not an invariable rule with even the best of cow horses: some stop hard and are difficult to sit, turning. When an obstacle confronts a horse running in rough ground, it breaks up his stride, often making the rider feel as though he were being torn into several pieces. You experienced nothing of this kind with Silver. He would simply change his lead, slipping into another gait or combination of gaits, selected by himself out of his vast repertory of paces. This mixing and sliding in and out of gaits is one of the pet aversions of the show ring judges, who judge horses according to show standards; but in actual practice the horse himself knows best. Silver would, by a clever manipulation of stride, bring you down a rocky hillside after a cow as easy as running on the level.

He was the only cowhorse I ever rode that could be in more than one place at the same moment. In corralling a bunch of cattle, he would crowd both ends and the center simultaneously. Or so it seemed. You never needed to touch a line (rein); he would take complete charge, and woe to the animal that tried to break back past him; Silver's teeth were sharp.

It was this combination in him of power and agility that made him the best horse for roping in the open of my experience. Every cowhand knows that in this operation the "jump off" is the most important thing. If you can get on top of an animal before he begins to dodge and twist, roping is a simple enough business. Silver was plumb on top the first jump. It was a lovely thing to put this little horse to catch a calf running loose on the outside. He did everything except throw the rope.

On the road it was his habit to pass from one easy gait to another to suit his own sweet fancy, like a musician trying out different tunes on his instrument. Full of energy as he was, with saddle on and the bridle dropped I could depend on his staying in any place I left him till the cows came home. Once he was through with after breakfast highjinks, a lady could ride him. I remember a picture of him with my wife in the saddle and her baby on her lap. A thoroughly tame and domesticated example of mustang blood, I hear the reader remark. But wait.

One day I rode him into our little town of Wagon Mound five miles away. Having a good deal of business, I pulled off his saddle and bridle and turned him loose in storekeeper Adler's corral. It happened someone left the gate open and Silver slipped out onto the street. I at once borrowed a saddle horse, thinking to have no trouble in putting him back into the pen. But the only sight I got of Silver was him sailing over the nearby hill top in the direction of the Piedra Alumbre, a wild mesa lying east of town. During the next few days I saw him and made several attempts to get him back inside our fence, but the instant he'd catch sight of me he'd start off with mane and tail flying, looking back over his shoulder at me as though he were mocking me. He made a fine sight. Three centuries of unbridled liberty were in that stride of his. I have always maintained that the movement of an unbitted range bronc had an element of freedom in it the most highly finished show bench animal doesn't exhibit. Finally he disappeared altogether and I heard no more of him till after many weeks later Dolf Harmon who rode for the Red River Cattle Company wrote me that he was running over towards their pasture on Red River, (which is what in those days we called the upper Canadian.)

So over to Dolf's camp in the Red River breaks I went one evening and that night we planned to take out Dolf's mount of saddle horses and try and get Silver to join in with them and so get him into the corral. Sure enough next morning there was Silver all by himself out on a high point of the Piedra Alumbre. We turned Dolf's remuda loose and hid ourselves. Mighty circumspectly Mister Silver circled around for a while and finally joined it. Then, having allowed him a spell to get on terms with his new mates, we, likewise mighty circumspectly, rounded the bunch up, greatly tickled to find that Silver showed little signs of wanting to break away. Indeed he acted as though he were tired of being alone and was glad of companionship. Very shortly we had him in Dolf's corral. He was hog fat and evidently plenty salty. Dolf seemed to be looking forward to his putting on a show when we saddled him up, but I gave him very little chance to act up, although, believe me, a feller needed to be greased lightning, mounting, when that little horse was feeling like that.

We kept Silver till he died a number of years later, but he never got a chance to make another breakaway.

SOME RECOLLECTIONS
OF A
WESTERN RANCHMAN
NEW MEXICO, 1883-1899

BY

THE HON. WILLIAM FRENCH

CAPTAIN French went to the Far West in 1883 to better his fortune. His adventures before and after he settled down to cattle-ranching in New Mexico make excellent reading. He writes of the trials of a tenderfoot, of the Indian Wars, of broncho-busting and rounding up mavericks, of sudden killing and rough justice, in a spirit of genial reminiscence, with a love for a good story. Even when he became an employer his troubles did not cease, as this amusing and exciting book shows.

METHUEN & CO. LTD. LONDON

Back cover of William French's book, *Some Recollections of a Western Ranchman*, 1928.

80

Captain William French

William French was born in Ireland in 1854 and served in the British Army from 1876 to 1882. After resigning his commission, he travelled to California having heard about mining opportunities in the American West. Next, he was drawn to the ranching frontier of New Mexico and in 1884 joined fellow Brit Harold Wilson on his WS Ranch located in the rugged southwestern part of the Territory. The WS Ranch was in the path of raiding Chiricahua Apaches who swept through the country during the first years he managed the ranch.

Aside from depredating Indians, ranchers in the area suffered from the scourge of cattle rustling. Wilson was so impacted that he decided to move his herd in the late 1890s to grazing land that he bought from the Maxwell Land Grant Company in Colfax County north of Cimarron. The ranch's cattle were first driven two hundred miles to the Santa Fe Railroad shipping yards at Socorro, shipped north to Springer and subsequently driven to pastures of the new WS Ranch.

In the 1920s while in retirement in California, French wrote his memoirs of life on the WS that were published as *Recollections of a Western Ranchman*. In the stories included here he recounts an episode he witnessed when an unlikely looking stranger rode an outlaw horse, a theme of stories told on ranches all over the West. Also, he describes a humorous story of the counter branding of his ranch's cattle by a neighbor.

Recollections of a Western Ranchman
Silver City: High Lonesome Books, 1997
Original title: *Some Recollections of a Western Ranchman 1883–1899*

"Horse Breaking and Cattle Raising"

A message came from one of the hands that they were breaking horses in the round corral, and that they had an old gentleman who had come in the evening before with a butcher's knife stuck in his boot who claimed he could ride, and the boys had christened him, 'The Granger,' and he thought they were going to have some fun with him.

I sent down word that I was busy writing, but that I would come as soon as I could, and then proceeded to get busy and tried to forget all about them. I had not proceeded very far, however, when the yips and yells coming from the corral sadly disturbed me, and I was tempted on to the porch to see if I could get a glimpse of what was going on. The walls of the corral were fully eight feet high, but I could see the form of the rider, and occasionally the back of the horse, appear and disappear at frequent intervals over it. Sometimes the back of the horse appeared without the rider, and then the cheering and yelling redoubled in volume, a sure indication of the failure of the rider to retain his seat.

I watched it for a minute or two, and then the temptation proving too strong, I let the correspondence slide and getting my hat hurried down to join them. The horse corral had large double gates facing each other, one opening into a series of picket corrals and the other leading into the open. Through the former the broncos were introduced to be saddled and broken, and when duly calmed were led out through the other and into an enclosure which contained the stables.

When I got down there, there were two or three in the corral in various phases of being roped and saddled with their prospective riders attending to them. The rest of the outfit were seated on the gate or in its neighborhood, and amongst them I recognized the gentleman who had been christened 'The Granger.' He was a middle-aged man and a typical tramp from his battered hat to his run-down boots, with the handle of the butcher's knife sticking out of the top of one of them.

He didn't appear to be particularly interested in the proceedings, or indeed in anything else, and to the frequent invitations to get down and show what he could do merely jerked the tobacco juice out of his mouth and intimated that he was waiting for something that needed riding. The general belief was that he was merely bluffing, and after a time the boys took little or no notice of him.

The lot that were in at the time I came on the scene were fairly tractable and were duly ridden and led out to make room for the next batch. Amongst the latter was a big bay horse they called Bullet which at one time had been partially broken, but having got away and run wild amongst the mares he had proved difficult to catch and was for several years conveniently forgotten. He was now over eight years old and Fred (WS ranch foreman) had determined to make use of him, so this time he was duly rounded up and took his place amongst the colts.

All hands were eager to have a try at him, though most of them knew he was vicious, for I had related to Fred my experience of him, which had occurred before he came to the WS. When he had been brought in as a three-year-old and escaped they had bobbed his tail and I, on one of my excursions after the mares, seeing his bobbed tail had mistaken him for one of the regular saddle horses. With great difficulty I had succeeded in corralling the whole bunch in a corral on the Thomason Flat, some miles from the ranch.

Here, single-handed, I managed to separate him from the others and turned them loose. Then having got him alone in the corral I proposed to rope him and lead him back to the ranch. My rope was rather short, but I managed to get it on him without difficulty and then proceeded to lead him. This was an entirely different matter, and to my astonishment he dragged me around the corral for fully twenty minutes. Thus failing to get rid of me and finding the tightening noose was beginning to choke him he changed his tactics and came at me open mouthed.

I barely escaped him by climbing the fence, and then had to run him to the ranch, where in order to recover my rope we had to forefoot him. After which we gladly turned him loose. Since then, which was some three years earlier, he had been unmolested, as, although he had been brought to the ranch several times and some feeble attempts made to handle him, he had always proved too much for his captors, who generally connived at his escape.

There were three or four others of the same kidney, but none of them so notorious as Bullet. He came in towering over the two or three broncos which accompanied him and really looked magnificent as he snorted and pawed the ground as if to show fight. The boys discreetly let him alone while the others were being thrown and saddled, and having ridden them for a few jumps, none of them giving a remarkable display, they let them out.

Bullet was now alone, and he careered around the enclosure, stopping every now and again to snort defiance, and as soon as the riders came back they looked at him in doubt. Some were for throwing him, especially those who did not pretend to be riders. Others thought it advisable to throw him back in the bunch till they had more time on their hands. Everyone had forgotten about the old gentleman on the fence. He was still chewing tobacco and apparently not taking much interest in the proceedings.

Someone was about to open the gate when he held up his hand and asked what was the matter with the bay. He was told that he was a pretty bad caballo (horse), and they thought of tying a saddle on him and leaving him saddled up for a day before attempting to ride him. His only remark was to spit the quid out of his mouth, slip down off the fence, give a hitch to his old pants and say, "Hell! I'll ride him."

It took a minute or so for the observation to sink in, and then it was received with an ironical cheer. At first nobody thought he was serious, but when he borrowed a pair of spurs from Fred and proceeded to buckle them on it began to dawn on us that he really meant to ride him.

Some caustic remarks were addressed to him in regard to his will and his choice as to the mode of curia, but of these he took no notice, merely indicating with his hand to go ahead and get the saddle on. The proud Bullet was forefooted, and busted so hard that it broke his front teeth. Then it took all hands to hold him while he was hobbled fore and aft with the usual slip knot. A hackamore and blind were placed on his head and a saddle securely fixed before he was allowed on his feet.

When he got up, although blindfolded, he still looked defiant, the more so on account of the blood from his broken teeth. He did all that a horse can do to get rid of the saddle, but with men holding on to a rope from either side he gradually quieted down. Taking advantage of the pause the old man crawled on to his back, the blind was removed from his eyes, and we all ran to climb the fence and witness his demise. For a moment or two Bullet stood still with surprise, and then realizing that something was on his back, he turned himself loose. He pitched as only a Western bronco can pitch, with his head almost between his hind legs and his back arched. He sprang into the air fully five or six feet, reversing his position in the process and keeping it up in quick succession, till it looked as if his rider's head must have been shaken loose from his body. We all looked for both man and horse to come down in a heap, but they maintained their respective positions.

When Bullet found he couldn't unseat him he fairly screamed with rage and went round and round the enclosure, alternately pitching and plunging, for fully ten minutes, when finding it necessary to slacken his efforts in order to regain breath, he broke into a trot and eventually came to a halt. This gave his rider a chance to settle himself more firmly in his seat and prove to the maddened beast that he was his master.

The old fellow drove the spurs into him, and taking off his old hat, which had been pressed down on his ears, he slapped him with it in the face. This not having the desired effect, he reached down to the ground and seizing a handful of sand rubbed it in his steaming nostrils. Bullet was not prepared to stand much of that kind of work, and after making a futile effort to kick him like a cow, threw down his head and commenced his pitching. He went through the same performance for another ten minutes and with the same result, this time coming to a stand with a regular scream.

At first we had looked on with astonishment and incredulity depicted on our faces, but when we realized that the old fellow really could ride the cheering that we gave him made the whole place ring. When they came to a halt after the second round the old fellow himself was glad to take a breather, but he made no attempt to dismount, merely remarking, "He sure is a daisy."

Then it was suggested that he should take him outside, and everyone who had a horse saddled there got ready to accompany him, prophesying that by the time they got back Bullet could be thrown into the regular remuda. The gates were thrown open, and seeing a chance for liberty, he went through them like a shot, proving that he had been correctly named. He was joined on the outside by all the boys who were mounted, and they went off 'hell for leather,' as if the devil was behind them.

I followed on foot, determined to see all I could, but they had not gone more than fifty or sixty yards when Bullet, to show he was still in the ring, threw down his head and renewed his pitching. This time he had the whole world before him and his efforts, if possible, exceeded anything he had done in the corral. The yipping and yelling went on for a minute or two and the old man seemed fairly comfortable, but all of a sudden, I saw him sway in his seat and slip round to one side under the animal's feet.

The saddle had turned, and it looked as if the infuriated animal must trample him to death. I ran up as fast as I could, and all the boys had pulled up and were forming a circle round him. He was equal to the occasion, however, for on going over he managed to get hold of the noseband of the hackamore and was holding on for grim death with a hand on each side of the animal's jaws. In this way he managed to keep his head and body off the ground while his feet were still in the stirrups with the spurs hooked into the broad hair cincha and over the animal's back.

The infuriated brute, being unable to bite him, was endeavoring to rake him off with his front feet. How long the struggle might have gone on it was impossible to say, but for the minute or two that it lasted it looked as if it could only have one end, and that we would be compelled after all to consign the old gentleman to a decent grave. He couldn't have held on much longer, when Fred, with great presence of mind, rode up as close as he could to the plunging brute and, seizing a favourable moment, pulled out his gun and shot him through the head just under the ear.

He dropped in a heap like a bundle of clothes, and, to our great relief the old man rolled out from under. He was not in the least flurried. His first care was to shake his foot loose from the cincha, after which he helped himself to a chew of tobacco, got on his feet, and looked at Bullet for some time without comment or remark of any kind. It was apparent he was quite dead, and seeming satisfied he pushed him with his foot, said he was 'a likely kind of a hoss,' and proceeded to undo the cincha.

We all congratulated him on his escape, but he didn't seem to notice it—just said it was a pity to have to kill him—and we all pitched in and rolled him over to free the saddle. That was the end of poor Bullet.

His late rider shouldered the saddle and blankets and we all marched back to the corral. He was offered his choice of the mounts on the ranch, but he said he wasn't interested, and after he had sat long enough on the fence to recover his breath he went back to the house, and that was the last that I saw of him. I never learned his name, nor where he went, nor where he came from. He was just an incident that came into my life, but made himself sufficiently interesting to be remembered.

About this time, in the year 1895, there was really beginning to be some demand for cattle. There were rumors of people being in the country and desirous of contracting for their purchase several months in advance of the date of their delivery and paying substantial sums down to bind the contract. All this was very encouraging to the cattle owner, but it also brought about the revival of the rustler. He sprang again into existence with the rise in the price of cattle. The Indian outbreak, which had been the original cause of his disappearance, had been followed by a period of depression which had lasted ten years and rendered his calling un-remunerative; but now he came again like a field of mushrooms after a warm rain. It was an ancient, and at certain periods of history by no means a dishonorable, profession, and from my experience of the New Mexico operators I would judge that the tricks of the trade had been handed down to them in unbroken succession.

Due to the revival of this industry recent legislation had been initiated in the Legislature at Santa Fe which led to the creation of the Cattle Sanitary Board. The registration of brands was now removed from the jurisdiction of the county clerk and placed in the hands of the newly established board.

Beyond this, the law also contained a clause making the acceptance and record of a brand, by the secretary of the board, in itself *prima facie* evidence of ownership in any court of justice. This clause was of great assistance to the legitimate owner, as, naturally, the nefarious gentleman, whose only title was a running iron, was not anxious to expose his delinquency by recording his name and address with the Cattle Sanitary Board. Consequently, when a new brand showed up on the range of which nobody knew the owner an application to the Sanitary Board to record it in your name, if not already recorded, gave you a certain legal right to bar it out and replace it by the brand of the legitimate owner.

The favorite method of those gentlemen of acquiring a herd without the preliminary expense of paying for them was what was known on the range as 'sleepering the calves.' Sleepering was simplicity itself and merely consisted of catching the animal before it left its mother and marking it with the legitimate ear mark of its owner while neglecting to go through the formality of branding it. It was a simple process and occupied little time, after which one turned it loose and invoked the guardian angel of the rustlers to preserve it from detection until in due time it became old enough to leave the maternal care and become a genuine maverick (unbranded and unclaimed).

Having reached this stage with the knowledge of its location and general appearance, it was up to the rustler to catch it before anyone else detected that it was unbranded; then he could decorate it with his own brand, or if not already in possession of one, with one invented for the occasion. Then a few dexterous snips with a sharp knife altered the original ear marks, and there was the foundation of a new herd. That we had to contend to a large extent with this evil may be inferred from the fact that amongst the archives of the WS Ranch are to be found the record of over seventy brands, recorded by me with the Cattle Sanitary Board during a period of some eighteen months, all of which showed up on the range and were intended to cover the WS brand.

In a rough country like ours this sleepering was difficult to detect. It was generally done amongst the outside cattle which clung to the mountains, and after a hard day's ride it was excusable for one not to risk his neck should an ear marked calf jump up in front of him, even though he actually did not see the brand. Then even in a roundup, which usually contained several thousand cattle, where it was the custom to start by cutting out the cows and calves that needed to be branded, in the dust and confusion a calf that was ear marked, though unbranded, could easily be overlooked. Also, which was generally the case, the author of the sleepering was pretty sure to be at the round up, and if he came in contact with his quarry on the drive it was a certainty that it would not reach the round up ground.

The brands showing up on our range, the majority of which were to be utilized in covering the WS, I naturally recorded as fast as they showed up, and this summary proceeding naturally led to friction with the independent gentlemen who created them. Amongst them was a rather amusing encounter with a gentleman named Holoman.

His given name was Tuk, and I have never been able to ascertain what it stood for. He was one of three brothers who migrated into our country from Texas impelled by the advancing tide of civilization and its accompanying inconveniences.

The oldest brother was Bob, who had in his possession few head of cattle, some eight or ten, probably strays as they were profusely ornamented with brands. Bob was a genial soul, in the language of the country "foot-loose,' meaning that he was unmarried and had no encumbrances to hamper his profession. This he openly stated to be that of a rustler or cow thief, and he didn't give a cuss who knew it. Our personal relations were devoid of malice, and we regarded each other with a mild admiration such as might be exchanged between an inspector of police and a distinguished burglar.

Tuk was the second brother and a victim of family cares. Though his profession was similar to Bob's, he did not openly assert it. He was a furtive individual and preferred to do his stealing in the dark. He rode wide when he saw you coming, and if compelled to pass closer gave you a furtive look and somewhat hostile greeting, which induced you to look behind and see that he was not taking an unfair advantage of your position. He claimed no cattle on his first arrival, no doubt being too busy with his domestic duties to be an assistance to Bob. The third brother was Pad, presumably an abbreviation for Patrick, who was a youth of about eighteen on his arrival and gave his services impartially to the general welfare of the clan.

They settled down in Alma and were not long before making their presence known on the range. It was a disadvantage to Tuk that he owned no cattle, but he apparently had a little money and was able to overcome the difficulty of acquiring the ownership of a few head, the remnant of a brand that had been started by a man named George Roberts. The Roberts boys had purchased a small bunch of cattle from a man named Bob Hanner, who had driven them in from Texas. Bob's real name was Stuart, but as certain authorities in the latter state had been making inquiries about him, he preferred to be called Hanner.

We were glad when the Roberts boys purchased his cattle, for Hanner had adopted for his brand a WN with a bar under it, from which he hoped to derive great profit as it covered the WS. To make this clear

I might mention that on the range where the brands were put on with a red-hot iron, curves were more in favor than angles. The latter, owing to the proximity of the irons, were difficult to put on with a stamp iron without causing an unsightly blotch and sometimes disfiguring the brand so as to make it impossible to read it.

The WS brand was therefore at this time, and as it had been originally recorded, put on with what was known as a running W. Mr. Hanner also adopted this form, only instead of following it with an S, he adopted the letter N, which also, as he said, for fear of disfigurement, he preferred in its running equivalent. Now, it did not require an expert to see that the S could easily be converted into an N by the prolongation of either end, and as for the bar underneath it could be produced by means of a running iron or numerous other methods unnecessary to mention.

However, he had only evolved this little scheme a short time before the coming of the Roberts boys. I had intended making a protest to the Sanitary Board when the brands were transferred, but when the Roberts boys got hold of it they relieved my anxiety, for the brands having to be newly recorded in order that they should know the ones actually in existence, they agreed to transfer the brand specifically to the right side, which removed it from conflict with the WS, which was always on the left.

The Roberts boys were nice straight boys, and as long as they were in the business our relations were of the best; but the hard times gave them a distaste for the business and they gradually disposed of most of their herd. They had but a few left at the time of the arrival of the Holomans, probably not over twenty or thirty head, and these they got rid of to Tuk Holoman, selling them at range delivery for a nominal sum.

Tuk soon got on to the lay of the land and thought it a pity to waste such a good opportunity. Ignoring such trifles as the records of the brand, he began to brand his increase on the left side. The first of them I saw really belonged to one of his cows, but I remonstrated with him. His excuse was that he was so accustomed to looking on the left side of the animal he paid no attention to what was on the right.

This not sounding convincing and my further protest being unavailing our relations became strained. I wrote to the secretary of the Sanitary Board and asked if it was permissible to record the WN bar brand on the left side, informing him of the circumstances which led to my making the request. His reply was that it was already recorded on the right side, but he didn't see any objection to its being recorded again on the left, and at any rate he would hold it in abeyance till the meeting of the board and would accept no other record in the meantime.

As a matter of fact they did actually record the brand on the left as belonging to the WS, but I did not wait for their certificate, as I considered I had enough to go on. The first calf I met with Tuk's brand on the left side after that I barred out and transferred it to the WS. This led to open warfare, and threats were conveyed to me from several quarters as to what Tuk was going to do with me.

I was not disturbed by Tuk's threats—had it been Bob I would have been more uneasy. But I did have some misgivings as to the legal aspect of the steps I was taking, and I made several efforts in an indirect way to run on to him and see if we couldn't settle the matter amicably, but he always avoided me. One day when I had almost forgotten about him and his cattle, I ran on to him unexpectedly.

I had been out inspecting some corrals that needed repair near the head of the Kellar Canyon and had heard a shot but paid no particular attention to it, thinking one of the boys had seen a deer and shot it. However, as I rode a little farther, I met Tuk face to face coming round a corner. I naturally pulled up and so did he, and after eyeing each other for a brief moment, he jumped off his horse and pulled his gun out of the scabbard attached to his saddle.

I had no idea that he meant to use it, for I was totally unarmed. The carrying of a long forty-five and belt full of cartridges had never appealed to me. It was not only cumbersome and interfered with your work, but you were much safer without one. Situated as I was, in constant conflict with a certain element over scrupulous in their interpretation of the law, I was much safer to be unarmed. The plea of self defense might be easily established against an armed foe, but the assassination of an unarmed man was contrary to the ethics of the border and liable to be summarily dealt with. So with that, on the whole, I was not greatly disturbed by Tuk's manifestations.

He was in a truculent humor, however, and demanded that I get down and fight him. This appeal to arms seemed rather one sided, and I pointed out the disparity of our weapons, also demanding to know what he thought we were fighting about. He said I was robbing him of his cattle, and I retaliated that my sole desire was to prevent him robbing us of ours. He had no reply to make to this but said that he wanted the thing settled once for all and that the present moment seemed to be as propitious an opportunity as he was liable to get.

I agreed with him as to the time and place, saying that if he would put up his gun, I had no objection to fighting him with fists. He sized me up pretty closely before replying, but seeing that I was stripped to my shirt and pants and had no means of carrying a concealed weapon he put his gun back in the scabbard on his saddle. He also took off the pistol belt and scabbard and hung them on the horn of his saddle. I wasn't much stuck on the encounter, but it seemed a ground hog case, so before dismounting I suggested that the loser should withdraw all opposition, and that if he called for time first he should make no further attempt to brand his cattle on the left side, and I, on my part, would lay no further claim to any of his calves.

This seemed to suit him, and I got off my horse thinking I was in for a long and doubtful battle. To my surprise and relief, however, it only lasted one short round. He came at me with a rush swinging his arms like an old fashioned windmill, made one wild swipe, which I dodged, and retaliated with a not very vigorous left to the nose as the force of his swing brought him past me. I had not struck very hard and must have had my hand rather loose, for it knocked down one of my knuckles and it has remained down ever since.

Harmless as I supposed it was, it was enough to finish the battle. It had drawn first blood and, much to my relief, Tuk threw up his hands declaring that he perceived that I was scienced and might as well give in before he got hurt. He pronounced it 'skienced,' and though I was pleased to see him surrender, it was some time before it dawned on me what he meant.

As we rode home together, he was rather depressed, and as the trail was rough in places, I allowed him to ride a little in front. As we jogged along, I got to thinking over the events and wondered if my estimate of Tuk had not been doing him an injustice. I reflected that he might have made use of his gun, and even if he did not assassinate me might have forced me under stress to accord him more favorable terms. With those thoughts in my mind I resolved to let him know before we parted how much I was indebted for his chivalrous conduct.

Our way led apart two miles from the ranch, and as I rode alongside him, I began to express my appreciation in a somewhat awkward manner. He had eyes like a ferret, and he looked at me piercingly, under the impression, as he expressed it, that I was 'giving him a game.' Then seeing that I really meant it he quickly disabused me of the notion by declaring, "Why, hell! I didn't have no cartridge."

He looked so despondent and his regret at the deficiency as so sincere that I burst out laughing. He explained in regretful accents that he had started out with only two or three cartridges in the magazine of his gun, and these he had expended in an unsuccessful attempt to shoot a deer, no doubt the one I had seen cross the canyon. He said he pulled the gun under the impression that he was going to run a bluff and make me withdraw from my position, but I was apparently so unperturbed that he supposed I had caught on and there was no way out of it except to fight.

He was really heart broken, not so much at losing the fight as that his belt was unfurnished with ammunition. He was also afraid, as he expressed it, that he might have to quit the country. As he explained it, he said that as soon as I had told how he had come to change his brand the boys would never let up on him but would devil him out of the country. His main grievance seemed to being reduced to fighting with his fists instead of his gun, and to relieve my mind, I said there was no necessity to say anything about it.

This view of the matter brought him unexpected relief, but he did not seem at all confident that I would adhere to it. I, however, reassured him to the best of my ability, and he left me apparently satisfied. Up to this time I have never mentioned the episode, and he, on his part, though never what might be called a satisfactory neighbor, confined his brand strictly to the right side of his cattle.

Colonel Jack Potter

Colonel Jack Potter

Colonel Jack Potter, affectionately known as "Lead Steer" Potter, was born in Caldwell County, Texas in 1864. At age sixteen he signed on with a trail herd destined for the Kansas rail shipping point of Dodge City. While in the Indian Territory, he fell violently ill and was forced to return home.

In the spring of 1882, he hired on to the New England Livestock Company and subsequently went north with three of the company's herds to railheads in Kansas. Afterward, he was sent by the company to the Pecos River in New Mexico Territory to take charge of the company's breeding ranch headquartered at Lucien Maxwell's old ranch at Fort Sumner.

He continued in their employ until the company liquidated in 1893. Afterward he went into the cattle business for himself at the Escondido Ranch in the Dry Cimarron Valley northwest of Clayton in Union County. He retired from ranching in 1928 and moved to Clayton where he later served several terms in the New Mexico Legislature.

He wrote many stories about his experiences on the New Mexico range that were published in the *Union County Leader*, *New Mexico Magazine*, and other periodicals. His stories were compiled into two books, *Cattle Trails of the Old West* (1935) and *Lead Steers* (1939). In the story included here he relates the heroic tale of his faithful and sagacious lead steer, Lew Wallace.

Cattle Trails of the Old West
Clayton: Leader Press, 1935

"Trail Dust"

Hoodoo Johnson and I fixed up a swell dugout camp at Mora Springs, forty miles southwest of Fort Sumner, when our outfit sent us out to a line camp on the edge of the range after the roundup in '87.

We went about our regular routine of riding the line, cutting for sign, and watching for cattle tracks in bunches or small droves that might be driven off and taken to Fort Stanton for slaughter. In January, a blizzard set in, and we were snowbound.

It was the second day of the blizzard, about midnight, I think, when I heard cattle lowing and coming down from off the ridge. I was afraid of a cave-in on our dugout if they happened to walk on the roof, so I woke up Hoodoo.

We started a fire and lighted the lanterns. When we looked out we saw hundreds of cattle bunched up around our camp and up and down the arroyo under the gip bluffs. They probably had drifted for miles looking for a windbreak.

Hoodoo seemed kind of peeved about the cattle drifting in.

"Next spring there'll be about ten thousand drift cattle in the Capitans and the same on the Rio Hondo," he grunted. "There'll be plenty of cutting and slashing for us cow servants when these critters have to be separated from the southern herds one at a time and trailed back to their home range."

And with that he went to bed. I put the coffee pot on the fire, making up my mind to stay awake as long as the drift herd remained around our camp. I was nodding a couple of hours later when I heard the lead cattle lowing and starting up the south slope. Then I heard the lowing of cows and the answer coming back from the calves near camp.

After a bit it seemed the herd had moved on and everything was quiet. I must have been half asleep when I heard sharp raps on the door.

I grabbed for my forty-five and jumped up at the same time. I listened and thought I must have been hearing things in a dream. Then there was a scratch on the door. I waited, and it was repeated. "Come in," I said. All quiet.

"Hoodoo," I shouted, "get up quick. Things are in a mess around here. Someone rapped on the door, and I said, 'come in'—and nobody answers."

Hoodoo rolled out, picked up his forty-five, and sat down on the box. The lantern was between us, and we sat there with guns pointed at the door for—what, we didn't know.

"Do you think it is a ghost?" Hoodoo whispered.

"It might be," I said and thought of the superstition of the native people that the spirits of Billy the Kid, Tom O'Folliard, and Charlie Bowdre driving cattle off on the drift, and of the name given these drift herds, "El Partido de Las Animas," the herd of the spirits or herd of the devil.

In that dugout ghosts and spirit herd were not to be taken lightly.

"Do you know we are right on the old Fort Stanton trail where the Kid used to trail his stolen cattle?" I asked.

Hoodoo was cool, even with the possibility of ghosts standing outside the door.

"It is claimed a ghost never harmed anyone," he said. "But I'm afraid it is the devil. He might be keeping up the rear end of that herd and might want to come in and warm his feet."

"Hoodoo," I said. "You have the wrong conception of the devil. I have always been told he is a hot piece of furniture and always works up in the lead instead of the drag."

Hoodoo started to say something, but there was another scratching on the door. Then there was a dull, rumbling "Moo-oo-oo."

"Wait a minute," Hoodoo gulped. He left his box and got his boots.

"If I die, I want to have my boots on."

Then we edged up to the door and after a minute of indecision jerked it open.

There stood a huge black steer with the longest pair of horns I had ever seen. His eyes were big and wide and the light from the lantern reflected back. We just stood there looking at our "ghost." We both felt just about as cheap as any two waddies (cowboys) could.

"Well, I looked for the worst," Hoodoo said. "Nothing could have surprised me. I always was a hoodoo for any outfit I ever worked for."

We closed the door and went to bed.

Next morning when I opened the door there was the big steer in the trench of our dugout door. I took out the nosebags for the horses and drove him away. When he followed me to the corral, I finally gave him a little grain, pouring it on the snow.

When he had eaten it he begged for more. He had my curiosity aroused, so I gave him a little more and studied him more closely.

"Well, old fellow," I said when I noticed a "32" on his neck. "This is the old county brand for Gillespie County, Texas. And here's NOT for the Knott Brothers who raised you. And here's SL for Shriner and Lytle. It's a road brand and shows you were sold to them and trailed north.

"And here on your hip you've got a WO which shows you were sold in Indian Territory to Doctor Brown and then sold to the New England Livestock Company and trailed to Fort Sumner.

"Your last brand, FHC. Well, old fellow, I know you now. You were Tom York's lead steer. I have heard him talk about you. I'm an FHC puncher myself—and you're sure welcome here."

And he was. For the next sixty days this steer had his grain twice a day and was proud of his new home. He was both sociable and intelligent. I don't think I ever rode into camp, but what he didn't quit grazing and come to camp to welcome me.

Sometimes when I did not pay any attention to him, he would give me a little gouge in the ribs with one of his long horns, the same as to say, "Can't you notice a fellow?" I would scratch him between the horns which always pleased him.

One day I made up my mind to name him. I told Hoodoo I was going to call him Lew Wallace.

"What in the Sam Hill do you want to name him for a soldier for, instead of a cowman?" Hoodoo protested. "Why not call him Murdo Mackenzie or Phelps White or Jim Hinkle, after real cowmen?"

"Well, Hoodoo," I said, "you don't seem to know that Lew Wallace savied the cow business in this country. You should remember that the Lincoln County cattle war was on for almost two years and Governor Axtell could not cope with the combine and was recalled, and the President selected one of his ablest generals, Lew Wallace, and appointed him governor to handle the situation.

"When Lew Wallace took his oath he did not try to handle the way by giving orders from Santa Fe. He hired a buckboard and driver and went down to Lincoln. Then he got the two fighting factions together and laid down the law."

" 'I have come down here to stop this war,' he told them. "What are you fellows fighting for? You have neglected your herds and have not marketed your steers for two years. You have stopped immigration to this fine country. Many had gone elsewhere."

"I admire your fine citizenship, and I know you will reason and cooperate with me in setting this right. I have asked both factions to lay down their arms and forget about the war, and I will see that you are not punished."

"Well, everyone offered to surrender his arms except Billy the Kid. And you know the story of the Kid. He and a few others took up residence outside Lincoln County, and the name of Lew Wallace went down in history for quelling the Lincoln County War."

"I guess this steer's name is Lew Wallace, then," Hoodoo agreed. So our steer became Lew Wallace.

In March when we broke camp to head for Fort Sumner, I poured out a generous feed of corn for Lew Wallace, thinking I would not see him again until roundup time.

I was mistaken. He followed us right on into Fort Sumner.

Notice was sent to other ranchmen that the roundup outfits would leave Fort Sumner on the first day of April, heading south to the lower Pecos country to commence the steer roundup.

We loaded up the chuck wagon with a thirty-day supply and pulled to one side of the old ranch fort where there was a vacant building and camped.

Next morning when I got up, the cook had a big fire started and was preparing breakfast.

"Cocinero," I said, "Do you know this is April the first—all fool's day?"

We put vinegar into a whiskey bottle, mixed a little cayenne pepper with it, and set it on the chuck box table. I commenced waking those waddies up. They dressed and came out one at a time.

"These spring mornings sure do make a fellow feel ornery." I pointed to the bottle. "You had better whet up your appetite."

Well sir, the boys fought their heads, just like burros.

We had old Lew Wallace riled up, and he was standing there looking on.

Hoodoo came walking out, the last man. He saw the bottle setting there. "I don't care if I do," he said. Then he commenced throwing one fit after another and hollering. "I'm poisoned. I knew I was a hoodoo!" This seemed to tickle old Lew Wallace. You could see a large grin on his face.

After the boys had quieted down, I got hold of a large sour dough biscuit, opened it up, filled it with cayenne pepper and handed it to Lew Wallace.

He rolled it around in his mouth a time or two and swallowed it. Suddenly, he commenced circling around the wagon, pitching and bellowing, and sticking his tongue out. I felt like congratulating myself on my achievements in furnishing a little humor for the lonely cowboys, but later, I felt a little uneasy. When the boys were riding three or four abreast and talking low I couldn't help but think they were framing me.

That noon day I got off to one side and spread my slicker down under the shade of a hackberry tree. I always had the name of being a good sleeper and soon dozed off. I dreamed I could see thousands of cattle coming down the slope to water and not a branded one in the bunch. All mavericks! And while I was prowling, looking for a place to start my branding fire, I was awakened by several shots and could hear bullets flying by. I jumped to my feet with the powder smoke pouring out of the bosom and sleeves of my shirt and my face stinging from powder burns. There stood six of those waddies with smoking guns in their hands. I blinked. "I expect I'm shot all to hell," I said.

Then the whole darn camp went to rolling on the grass, laughing, and the old cook said, "Ain't this a great day?"

We traveled on, and arriving in a few days at the starting place of the roundup, divided our outfits so we could work in three divisions. About the fifteenth of May we all met at Fort Sumner and commenced cleaning up the herds, exchanging cattle, etc. At the roundup at Bosque Redondo, after the circlers had got in and our remuda was gathered near the roundup, I began wondering about Lew Wallace as this was supposed to be the final roundup, I began to think he had evaded the boys.

I was putting my saddle on my cutting horse when someone slipped up behind me and nudged me in the ribs. "Boo."

It was Lew Wallace greeting me. He went over to the other side and said howdy to Hoodoo. Then he moseyed off toward camp and ate all the cook's cold bread. When we went in to dinner he was lying nearby chewing his cud.

In the next three days large steer herds were shaped up and passed on with the regular percentage of cutouts, and we were ready for the drive.

It was an eighty mile drive to the Blue Holes watering place on the Pajarita, and the report of the puncher who scouted the trail was discouraging. But with Lew Wallace in the lead, we started the long drive at around noon after the herd had filled up on water. It is necessary that every animal, horse or steer be filled with water at the start of the drive, and they won't drink until about 11 a.m. to 1 p.m.

We got started with a herd that was so chuck full they were lazy and would not string out being much more content to graze. I worked them only about eight miles the first afternoon, had supper, and bedded the cattle down until midnight. Five hours' rest for everyone except the two guards.

At midnight we hit the trail. At daylight we were 20 miles out. The cattle were very hungry, so we grazed them for three hours giving all the boys not on herd a chance to take a nap, and then we took the trail, the cattle stringing out well.

We had an early supper, got our remuda watered, changed mounts, and sent the former ones off to water. We made our night drive in the early part of the night, stopping at the going off place on the plains forty miles out from the starting place.

Next morning the cattle still wanted to graze. We were glad to see this as real thirsty cattle will not graze. We nooned on Plaza Largo which was a dry creek forty-eight hours out and forty-eight miles away. It was a very warm day. I let the cattle and men rest there three hours and started on after eating supper.

We started a night drive and as the trail led in between some dry arroyos with steep banks and gullies, we got into trouble and had to bed down. Everyone rested but the guards, and they were relieved a time or two.

In the morning we were short of water. I went to the barrel to fill my canteen but changed my mind. There was Lew Wallace leading his herd sixty hours without water. A man would be a slacker that couldn't make it on through without water.

Right here we got balled up. I sent the wagon and horses off with one of the boys to get camp water and water the horses, and he got lost and didn't show up until dark.

When Lew Wallace led off the next morning, not an animal put his head down to graze. It seemed that Lew Wallace looked taller, and longer, and gaunter than I had ever seen him. While I was checking the lead cattle, Lew Wallace walked up and looked at me in a sarcastic way, as if to say, "It seems to me as if you had got us into a mess." I answered him in my mind that we were both alike. I was very thirsty myself.

At noon I bedded the herd down to rest and waited for the wagon. We were now seventy-two hours out. At one o'clock we started on the last short stretch to Blue Hole, the watering place.

A hot, strong wind came up which was a regular dust storm. Inhaling it in our dry throats was disagreeable. I told the boys to drop back along the line for fear the cattle would quit the trail. In a few hours we were going down the slope into Blue Hole. The trail hit the place angling down stream. Just as the lead cattle were passing the first trail down the bank, Lew Wallace dodged out. He and I went down the first trail and hit the water together.

First thing I knew we were out in water up to my horse's shoulder. I crawled off my horse and stooped over and tried to drink. I could not swallow.

When Lew Wallace had filled up he looked around at me, and he must have suspicioned something was wrong. He stood there and stuck his tongue out. So with my mouth full of tongue, I started throwing water with my hand. Finally I got so I could drink. When Lew Wallace thought I had enough he pushed me with his horn. We went up on the bank and cooled off, and after awhile we went down and finished our drink.

Time made by the lead cattle was 76 hours; by the drags, 79. There were no unusual hardships. Late in the afternoon when our entire herd had watered, we moved out to one side where the grass was fresh, and as soon as the cattle had satisfied their hunger, they bedded down and took a much needed rest.

We threw the herd next day at noon back into the water at the same place, and after finishing we hit the trail north. Our next trouble was too much water. After going on by old Liberty trading store, we crossed La Pajarita creek and turned pretty well to the east to Dead Man's Crossing of the Canadian. This was quite a detour. Fort Bascom was on our direct route, but as the north banks of the Canadian were steep and boggy, the trail herds had to abandon this crossing and had selected Dead Man's.

I rode down to the river and found it half bank full and rising fast. I galloped back to the herd and told the boys to rush the cattle, that if we did not hurry, I was a afraid we would not be able to cross the herd. There is nothing more unpleasant than to take your chuck wagon across a swollen stream.

We arrived at the stream. The water was still rising, but by a whole lot of persuasion, we got Lew Wallace to take the lead. He got half-way across in swimming water with the cattle following up nicely, when a drift log coming down stream at a rapid rate struck him in the ribs.

It must have knocked the breath out of him. He went down under the water, and when he came up had lost his bearings so he milled around once with the cattle and headed back toward home. I knew everything was off for the day. We drifted the cattle back out on the prairie and laid over until next day and crossed over successfully.

Our route took us up Los Carros creek, thence to Rincon Colorado, on to Ute Creek, thence up Ute Creek via Casa Blanca and on to where the Muerto empties into the Ute or Bueyeros, thence up the Muerto to its head, and thence to the crossing of the Tramperos near the old IL Ranch, thence to the Pinovitos at Clapham, on thence to Plum Grove on La Carriza, thence to Pitchfork ranch on the Perico.

After watering our herd and going back south out of the sand hills, we established camp. I and two other fellows that were interested in the herd washed our faces and put on our best clothes and pulled out to Clayton to make a survey of things around Clayton, such as getting camp ground close in, water for the remuda and corralling capacity of the stock pens.

I believe our herd was the first large herd offered for shipment out of Clayton as the grass in the yards had not been tramped out. We went on into Clayton, and I believe we received the greatest welcome I ever received in any cow town. The population had the Western spirit, everyone was a booster.

"Cow boss," they told me, "you have used great judgment in selecting this place for a shipping point. Every trail from the south or southwest leads to Clayton. You find here not only the fine water holes, but the shade and two kinds of gramma grass, and in this town you will find it inhabited with your kind of people. All cow people are welcomed here.

"Of course, we don't know that you gamble, but if you or your men do, you will find the best gambling tables in the West with no limit. Our saloon and gambling people are different from Abilene and Dodge City. They will not murder you when you are drunk. We are doing our best not to advertise this town by having a notorious Boot Hill. In a short while when cow people begin to know us, we will expect a continuous string of herds coming in from the south."

Well, I had a wire from Dupont and Green, who contracted for the herd, saying that they were having trouble getting cars, but that when they were sure the cars had been started out of Denver, they would come at once.

In a few days they arrived. I moved camp up next to the yards and commenced shaping up the cattle. The first train load was cut off from the herd and started to the corrals with Lew Wallace in the lead.

Cattle kept breaking back from the gate but after the third attempt we got them corralled. After loading them out, we took Lew Wallace back to pilot the other part of the herd. We soon got them corralled and then visitors commenced bragging about the cuteness of our lead steer.

Finally after loading about 30 cars I hurried off down to the depot to fix up some shippers' contracts for men that were going along with the cattle. As I was finishing the long train pulled down from the yard for orders.

While standing in the doorway near the second car from the engine, I heard a sad, mournful "Moo-oo." I recognized it at once as that of Lew Wallace's.

I walked up to the car and looked through a crack and there stood Lew Wallace, and he said "Moo" again. I said, "Jack Potter, what in the world do you mean by loading this steer? No Indian will eat him!" I told the engineer to cut out that car and back it to the yards for I wanted to unload my steer.

About this time the agent stepped out to give the engineer his orders and said, "It can't be done. This billing has been made out and handed to the conductor."

"I can't help it," I said. "You will have to mark on it 'one steer short.'"

About this time Dupont stepped up. "You can set your price," I told him. "I'm going to hold my lead steer. "What? Hold that lead steer?" he hollered. "I wouldn't take five hundred dollars for him. The Indian agent at Red Cloud always has trouble in corralling range steers, and he asked me to bring in a lead steer, and I have not been sleeping on the job."

"I am going to take Lew Wallace along and turn him over to that agent and tell him to keep him around, and shelter and feed him, and treat him as a lead steer should be treated. When he gets through with him, I will have a standing offer of $100 on him. When he dies with old age his horns will be worth that amount."

"Well, old hombre," I said, "you have made a good talk. Will you swear to that?"

"Certainly, I will," Dupont promised.

"Okay," I said to the engineer. "Get out of here pronto."

As Lew Wallace's car passed I bid him farewell forever. A dull, pitiful "Moo-oo-oo" echoed back. I could have sworn it sounded like adios.

Eugene Manlove Rhodes. (New Mexico State University Library, Archive and Special Collections)

EUGENE MANLOVE RHODES

Eugene Manlove Rhodes was born on a Nebraska homestead in 1869 and moved with his family to southern New Mexico Territory in 1881. At age thirteen he was hired as a horse wrangler on the Bar Cross outfit whose range extended along the Jornada del Muerto east of the Rio Grande. He subsequently worked for several neighboring outfits including the KY, KIM, 7TX and John Cross. During that time, he developed a reputation as an accomplished bronc rider and horse breaker. Among his entertainments were playing poker and baseball and fist fighting.

He also liked to read and was often seen reading a book while traveling horseback from ranch to ranch. His taste was wide reaching and included classic fiction and poetry that ranged from Dickens, Twain, and Keats. In 1888 decided on a college career and enrolled in the University of the Pacific in California. After two years of study, he grew so homesick for the New Mexico desert that he quit school and returned home.

In 1892 he homesteaded a ranch in the San Andres Mountains which were situated between the Rio Grande on the west and the Tularosa Basin on the east. He constructed a wagon road to his ranch up a canyon from the Tularosa side that was eventually named after him.

During 1899 he corresponded with a young woman, May Davison Purple, from New York State who had written him after reading some of the poems he had written for the college newspaper. They eventually married and bought a house outside of Tularosa where May lived, while Rhodes worked on the ranch in the mountains during the week. May's mother became ill in 1902 so the couple decided to move to Apalachin,

NY where she lived so that May could care for her. They lived there for the next twenty years.

Over that time Rhodes longed for the "big and barren desert country he called home" and eventually was inspired to write about it. The fiction he wrote was filled with vivid descriptions of life in the New Mexico cow country and the stark landscape where the cowboys, miners, and native inhabitants lived. His writing about range life, although fiction, is marked not only by its authentic descriptions of cow work but also by its fidelity to cowboy vernacular.

Most of the stories were published in serial form in the Saturday Evening Post. Many were subsequently compiled into book form with *Paso Por Aqui* (1927), *Bransford in Arcadia* (1914), and *Copper Streak Trail* (1922) being the most well-known. He wrote seven novels over the next twenty years during his exile in New York.

The Rhodes returned to New Mexico in 1926 and settled in Alamogordo. Four years later they moved to California because of Rhodes' health. He passed away there in 1934 but was later buried near his old ranch in the San Andres Mountains.

The following story is drawn from his book *West Is West* (1917). It is a representative example of how Rhodes captured the goings on of range life and its sights, sounds and smells.

West is West
New York: Grosset & Dunlap, 1917

"The Cutting Ground"

The "circle" gathers cattle as a drag-net gathers fish. The meshes of it are horsemen, a mile or two apart, according to the lay of the land. Each man is responsible for all cattle between himself and his next neighbor on either hand.

On the day the V Cross T drag had combed a little pear-shaped country with twenty-five miles as the shortest diameter. The program was, briefly: Breakfast before day; catch horses, a brisk ride of thirty-odd miles to the pear butt, divide and scatter, bringing all cattle to the appointed roundup ground by dinner time: dinner by sections, and change of horses; work the herd on the cutting ground through the long, hot afternoon.

In "working the herd," the horsemen, meshes of the forenoon, become a living fence; some become gates. The company men first, then each stray man in turn, goes through the herd and cuts out each his own.

Since noon the never ceasing feet had tramped the roundup ground to powder. The spring southwesters were blowing. The roundup was an impenetrable dust cloud from whose whirling center came rolling mutter and steady uproar—the complaint of a thousand protesting cattle.

Riders, dim-flitting, circled the herd; now seen, now blotted out; perhaps the cloud, thinning for brief space, gave a glimpse of bewildered eyes and crowding horns, white-flashing; to be swallowed up again in swirling tumult. From time to time there appeared on the cloud-edge a slow moving cluster of cattle from which a steer darted like four-footed lightning; lapped with him, nose to tail, a cutting horse in eager escort. They zigzagged in swift, unexpected angles like a water skipper gleaming to and fro over a sunny pool. Flashing, turning, as the steer tried to dodge back, the vigilant cow pony headed him off; still grumbling and garrulous, the steer hoisted his tail in token of defeat and made for the cut.

After cutting out the steers, the company calves were thrown into a separate cut and branded, then the stray calves cut out and branded; last, stray cattle were cut out, and finally all cuts thrown together and left in charge of a half dozen unlucky men until the day herd should come in. the range cattle were started off and turned loose, breaking up fan-wise across the sand ridges into the long, clamorous streaks, still running and bawling their sense of outrage to high heaven. The sun was low; already the day herd—huge, unwieldy—was slowly tumbling over the mesa's edge toward the bed ground. Close by, the wrangler was bringing the horse herd campward.

As the dust settled, little groups of men became visible, heading for the chuck wagon on the river bank, where in the lee of sheltering cottonwoods the cook's fire blazed brightly. Bridle on neck, the horses paced soberly, with much sneezing and shaking of wise heads; the horsemen brushing their hats, and removing the handkerchiefs tied over mouth and nose for protection from the choking dust. Last of all came the Cattle Inspector and Wildcat Thompson, deep in earnest converse.

The inspector had joined the outfit in the middle of the afternoon. The V Cross T had not seen him since the steer shipping of the West Work at Ridgepole, three weeks before—the day of the runaway freight car and the rehabilitation of Nate Logan.

"Say, Mr. Thompson," said the inspector, "there was a dogie in the pen up to your ranch and the feller there wasn't disseminating no information whatever. He said you was the editor of the question bureau—his business was to see that the stock got water and to blab yearlings; givin' out statistics to gratify idle curiosity weren't no part of his lay. He had all the symptoms of the malignant pip. So, I thought I would come down and see you. How about it!"

"Has it got a Hook and Ladder brand breaking out on it somewhere, and its ears cut bias?" queried Thompson lightly. "Cause if it ain't decorated that way, it sure ain't mine. I don't run but the one brand.

Wasn't that dust rank? Why, along about four o'clock a man on the far side of the herd might have stubbed his toe on the Rocky Mountains unbeknownst."

The inspector flushed. "Meanin' that if it wears your brand, it's yours, come hell or high water? Now, there's no use taking that tone, Steve. I ain't mistrusting you—stealing calves ain't your style. But there's the law. I got to see you prove that the dogie's mother was yours. You know the law as well as I do."

"No man shall keep a calf under seven months' old, unless he produce the mother on demand," quoted Steve soberly." "Or, should the said cow have the misfortune to be dead, he must have the last will and testament of the deceased, signed by two disinterested witnesses, settin' forth, in the name of God, Amen!—bein' of sound mind but failin' health, owin' to havin' been struck by lightnin', or eaten by bears, as the case might be, that she does hereby make, ordain, publish and declare these presents, to whom it may concern, to wit, namely; That she, the aforesaid cow, being owned by her owner, subject to first mortgage held by Citizen's Bank of Tucumcari, does hereby give, will, bequeath and devise to said owner, his heirs, executors and assigns forever, all her right, title and interest in the following named property, to wit: The undivided four quarters of one calf, located in the South East One Fourth of the South West One Fourth of the United States, and more particularly described in schedule A, as regards age, sex, color and disposition, and that she was rightfully and legally seized of said calf. Sure thing!" He paused for breath.

"Further," he recited glibly, "anyone violating the provisions of this act is liable, on conviction, to a term of eleven months in county jail or penitentiary, or a fine of five hundred dollars to one thousand dollars, or both. Oh, I know the law from A to Albuquerque! And the calf is sold for the Sanitary Board rake off—to pay for board meetin's and to carry elections with."

The inspector expostulated, "Oh, well now, what's the use of getting hot under the collar?" he said. "I suppose, of course, you can prove the dogie's mother was yours."

"Prove!" said Steve disdainfully. "Prove! You can prove anything— if getting two disinterested parties to swear to it, at five dollars per party, is any proof. I mind meetin' Jim Burleson in Lincoln once. Charged with stealing a span of mules, he was. "Hello, Uncle Jim! I sings out.

"How's your case comin' on?" "Oh, that's all right," he says. "That's all right! No trouble at all. Got it all fixed up. I can prove that I bought 'em by half a dozen good men. Jest one thing I am worried about; I don't know yet which span of mules it is!"

"Now look here, Steve," said the inspector protestingly. "Of course, I don't doubt that the calf's yours. I'm your friend. But I got to do my duty."

"Do your duty then. Who's hinderin' you?" said Steve. "But don't get mixed up none about what your duty is. You don't consider it anyways part of your duty to fine or imprison me yourself, do you? That takes a judge and jury. Nor to arrest me? It takes a sheriff and three drunk deputies to do that. That's what I elected a sheriff for—to look after such things for me. You ain't getting paid to arrest folks. You inspect, and if you see things anyways bent or curved-like, your duty is to report it. That calf isn't seven months old, its mother is dead as Melschisedk. I'm keeping it up and raising it on my old milk cow. I won't produce no witnesses to prove that its mother ever was mine. Why, if everybody had to prove they wasn't ownin' other folks' property, a title-deed wouldn't be no more good than a rain check in hell! Now go ahead and report, but don't you touch that calf!"

"You'll get yourself in trouble, Steve," warned the inspector. "What's the use of being stubborn? You don't want to defy the law. A good citizen ought to uphold it."

"Don," said Steve, more seriously, "a man that keeps a foolish law is only a fool, but a man who doesn't break a wicked law is knave and coward, or both, and fool besides. Your law is foolish; the open range don't average one man to every ten miles square. But cows die dead, whether you've got witnesses or not. It's hardly exaggeratin' to say they all die, sooner or later cows do. Leastways, I never seen none that didn't die once, sometime in their lives. And the rains don't begin till July, the calf harvest comes before that when the grass is shortest and driest; right then is when most cows die; it's exactly the cows with calves that have the best chance to die. You lose your cow by act of God, your calf by act of Legislature. You got no right to save the calf, unless you keep two disinterest witnesses under pay ridin' with you all the time.

"It's a wicked law. The Rio Grande is in flood, calving time; when it goes down, it leaves great stretches of mud and quicksand; the lakes are dryin' up, hundreds of cows bog down and die every day, leaving bright-eyed, pink nosed calves makin' anxious and pointed inquiries concernin' breakfast. 'Taint no difference whose they was. When a man finds one, he's either got to take it home across his saddle for the kids to raise or else shoot it. He can't leave the poor little trick to starve, a man can't, law or no law."

"Yes, but there's lots of thievin' goin' on," the inspector interposed. "Cuttin' young calves off from their mammies."

"Prove it, then, prove it and punish 'em," said Steve. "No self-respectin' cow thief 'ud do a thing like that. The union 'ud take away their cards too quick. Such dirt ain't man-size. If you prove it on me, give me all the law calls for, and take my tobacco. But don't try it without proof. I'll secede."

"This law proposes to put the burden of proof on the stoop-shouldered white man—make him prove he is innocent. Man wouldn't mind doin' that if he was guilty, but when he ain't, it annoys him. Talk about it bein' unconstitutional—why it's plumb unhygienic! It's contrary to bedrock principles of common law—and common sense, too, which is a damn sight more important. I got nothin' against you, Don, but when you send in your report, you give the Insanitary Board my best respects and tell 'em Wildcat Thompson says they can go plumb slap-dab to hell: that I keep this calf, that they can't find twelve men in the Territory that'll cinch me for not lettin' it starve, and if they fool with me one little bit, I'll fix 'em so their own dogs'll bark at 'em. Why, if they ever try to enforce such a pipe dream as that, I'll rip that board up into toothpicks! I'll plow Santa Fe up and sow it with salt; tourists in little black caps 'll be getting' off the Pullmans and inquirin' where the capital used to be!"

"Spare the women and children," implored the inspector." If, peradventure, there be any good men."

Wildcat grinned. "Shucks! No harm done as far as you and me are concerned. I got to catch my night horse."

The inspector spat thoughtfully as he unsaddled and turned his mount in the bunch. "Now," he soliloquized, "there is one man you could fall down and worship without sin—for there's nothing like him in heaven above or earth below or the waters under the earth. Of all the unruly, consarned, contrary critters!" Then a smile broke over his face. "I'm sure sorry for the Board!"

By the fire the busy cook hustled along the grub pile. The "Bobtail" guard had saddled their night horses and were off at a gallop to relieve the day herders and to bring the herd to the bed ground; to hold them there till the First Guard could eat supper and take the herd. The men who had started off the range cattle were riding back slowly; the low sun made their shadows long and thin behind them; the wind died with the dying day. The night wrangler and the First Guard had already caught and tied their horses and were eating "First Table." The Autocrat permitted this out of mere humanity, so they could go on duty and let the day wrangler and the Bobtail come into supper.

The inspector, deep in thought, watched the roping out of night horses. "Now Steve never stole that calf one single time," he pondered. "Some girl must have turned him down good and plenty for him to be cravin' to lock horns with the Cattle Sanitary Board just for the sake of entertainment and exercise. Myself, I wouldn't choose that form of excitement any. That's what I call goin' some."

ERNEST THOMPSON SETON

Born in England in 1860, Ernest Thompson Seton moved to Canada with his family at age six. After attending art schools in Toronto and London, he traveled to western Manitoba to homestead land with his brother. During his time there he became enamored with the wildlife on the plains, especially the birds, which he sketched and made notes regarding their behavior. He compiled the results of his work in a monograph titled *Birds of Manitoba* (1891).

After several subsequent years of art study in Paris, Seton arranged to go to New Mexico where he had contracted with a ranch owner to trap wolves that were depredating the man's cattle and sheep herds on his ranch in the northeastern part of the Territory. Seton arrived by train in Clayton in the fall of 1893 and began work on the L Cross F Ranch. After a few months he moved northwest to a camp on the Currumpaw River. There he successfully trapped many wolves, including a particularly notorious "outlaw" pack leader locally known as Lobo.

After leaving New Mexico, he wrote about the capture of the great wolf in a story titled "Lobo, The King of the Currumpaw." He put that story, along with one about a pacing mustang who ranged in the nearby San Carlos Hills into a best-selling book titled, *Wild Animals I Have Known* (1898).

While in New Mexico, he kept a journal filled with observations of wildlife and descriptions of the experiences he had with the cowboys, horses, and cattle on the ranches where he trapped. He included them in his autobiography, *Trail of An Artist-Naturalist*, that was published in 1940. Although he spent only a short time on the New Mexico range, his observations are insightful and vividly descriptive of the range men and animals he came to know.

Ernest Thompson Seton

Trail of an Artist-Naturalist
New York: Charles Scribner's Sons, 1940

"The Plains of the Currumpaw"

In the summer of 1893, I was invited to the New Jersey home of Louis Fitz-Randolph. Our conversation turned to his cattle ranch in New Mexico, and the terrible toll taken yearly by wolves. Fitz-Randolph said the cattle business would yield big dividends if he could curb those wolves, but they defied all the best efforts of cowboys, gunmen and trappers.

Oh, how I did long to go on a campaign against those wolves! I knew I could meet them and beat them, but I dared not take the time. My duties held me bound. I was working all day at the easel, and every night till late at my desk. The task was agreeable enough, and it all went in the direction of my ambition. But I was under a terrible handicap. Minute work, desk work, twelve and fifteen hours a day, was too much. Terrible excruciating pains were centered in my eyes. I tried different glasses. Finally, my doctor said, "Now, my friend, unless you wish to go totally blind, you will quit all desk and easel work and go for a long holiday in the wilds."

Then clear focus was given the thought by an offer from Fitz-Randolph. He said, "If you will go to my ranch in New Mexico, and show the boys some way of combating the big cattle-killing wolves, I will pay all expenses, and let you make whatever you can out of bounties and hides. But you must promise to spend at least a month on the ground at the work."

Thus, it was that on October 17, 1893 I left Toronto for Chicago enroute for Clayton, New Mexico, where my job was to hunt and destroy wolves, and show the cowboys how to do the same. My cash on hand was $80, supplied by Fitz-Randolph. Out of this, after paying $18.31 for ammunition, $34.65 railway fare, $10.41 for sundries including meals, I had remaining $16.83 to return to him.

I reached Clayton at 11 pm, October 22nd and put up at the Clayton House where reigned the genial proprietor, Harry Wells. On Tuesday, the 24th I got a thirty-mile lift with the mail carrier, Hubert Crouse, to Clapham post office, the nearest point to the Fitz-Randolph ranch, known locally as the L Cross F outfit.

Here I learned that, owing to the absence of the foreman, H.M. Foster, and the resignation of the cook, I was not to go to the head ranch on Penabetos (Penavetitos) Creek; but, by arrangement, board with one Jim Bender, a bachelor whose small holding was on the Leon Creek four miles northwest of Clapham. Bender was on hand with a buckboard for my baggage, and thenceforth he and I lived together in his lonely little ranch house.

Coyotes were plentiful. We saw two or three every day and heard many at night. Jackrabbits and prairie dogs abounded, but not a sign of a gray wolf did I see.

"No," said Jim, "we never see them in the daylight. If we did, we could kill them with a long-range rifle. But I'll show you lots of their work."

This he did, mostly the carcasses of yearling calves, with the hindquarters partly eaten, the rest left for coyotes and varmints.

Back of the ranch house, a quarter-mile, was a precipitous rocky hill known as Mount Tabor, named after a previous owner of the ranch. This was 200 feet high. One day I climbed it, and, in accordance with an old custom of the West, had built a stone obelisk to mark the highest point. Suddenly I noticed on the plain below me two coyotes, probably male and female, for they commonly hunt in pairs. I kept out of sight and watched them.

One coyote crouched behind a thick greasebush, the other walked openly toward a prairie dog that was yapping on its mound. He made a half-hearted rush as the prairie dog dived. The coyote far back behind the greasebush now rushed forward, and crouched beside a bush that was only six feet from the prairie dog hole. Meanwhile Coyote No. 1 was at a safe distance, and he was going still farther away. The yapper became bold; he stepped right out and yapped at Coyote No. 1. Coyote

No. 2 rushed forward and almost got him. In this case the trick failed, but obviously it must often be successful.

In Manitoba, the lasso is rarely seen; it is essentially a contrivance of the open range. My earliest sight of high-class lasso work was in Buffalo Bill's show.

But on arrival in the Southwest, one is soon struck by the fact that every horseman carries a coiled lasso hanging from the saddle horn; and the assumption is that every man can handle the lasso, and catch his horse at any time.

The second day at Bender's ranch Jim was going off about some distant business, leaving me at the table making a drawing. "Your horse is in the corral any time you want him," he said; and so he left me.

My sketch finished, I went out to saddle my horse. He was in the corral all right; but the corral was sixty feet across and perfectly round. I took the bridle in my hand, and went gently toward the animal, as I had done in Manitoba countless times. But this horse was of a different mind. No matter how I approached, he briskly avoided me; and there were no corners into which I might drive him.

I spent half an hour in vain. I could not get near him. How I did wish for some one who could throw the lasso! But I was absolutely alone and would be all day.

For lack of a better plan, I tried to remember how the lasso was usually thrown. I made the loop, and flung it awkwardly at the horse. Of course, I missed as far as catching was concerned. But the rope hung on the horse's neck and *he thought he was caught*. At any rate, remembering many previous catches, and rough handlings, my steed stood meek and trembling, and did not move out of his tracks. So I quickly bridled and saddled him.

That was absolutely my first throw of the lasso. Billy Allen was generally rated as the best roper in the region; and once or twice, he gave me some remarkable demonstrations. He could gallop alongside a steer and drop his lasso on any desired foot.

There is a strange malady known as "lumpy jaw" that affects range animals; that is, some minute parasite grows on the outer side of a beef animal's jawbone, causing a huge round swelling. It is not known to be infectious or poisonous, and yet animals so affected are declared "not fit to ship." Therefore, when seeking some beef for wolf bait, we usually sought out a "lumpy jaw."

One morning I said to Billy Allen, "I am out of wolf bait, and I see a big 'lumpy jaw' over in that far bunch."

"All right. Where do you want him killed?"

"I think that little draw between the two ranges of hills is a good place."

Accordingly, we cut out the "lumpy jaw" from his bunch and drove him to the selected spot. He was working up a fine rage and was very snuffy when we got him to the place.

"Keep back, and I'll throw him," said Billy. I held back in wonder, for the steer was more than twice the weight of Billy's pony. Billy galloped on the left side after the plunging steer. When close up, he threw the lasso over the steer's right shoulder so that it fell where the steer had to set his left foot in the loop. Billy jerked it tight, gave a sign to the pony, who at once threw himself back on his haunches; and the steer was thrown head down, hind legs up, with all the force of his own weight.

"Flank him!" yelled Billy.

I leaped from my horse, grabbed the low flank of the steer with both hands, set my knees against his back, and pulled with all my strength. At first the powerful brute lashed out with both hind feet, but I was able to hold him down, while Billy's horse held the lasso taut.

But, strange to say, as I held, his struggling died away. He lay at length perfectly still. Billy hurried to examine him and exclaimed, "Look! His neck is broken and both his horns."

In three minutes the steer was dead, with a broken neck and both horns broken off at the base, now hanging loose by their skin. Such is the power of a lasso throw, skillfully maneuvered.

(Note: One or two biological facts are of daily recognition on the cattle range. For example, a horse always rises forequarters first, a beef animal hindquarters first. Therefore, if you hold a horse's head on the ground, he cannot get up; or if a cattle beast's hindquarters are kept down, he cannot rise. When a roper throws a steer, and means to hold him down, he shouts to an assistant: "Flank him." This means that the assistant leaps from his horse, rushes to the downed steer, places his knees against the steer's back; and with both hands hooked onto the loose skin of the flank, pulls back with all his strength. This effectually prevents the steer from rising; he is absolutely controlled in this way, even if the lasso be removed from the horns or feet.)

I lost no time in beginning my wolf hunt. The wolves had killed seven colts and five sheep close to this settlement within the past three days. In the region was a wolf hunter named Joe Callis who had killed 109 gray wolves in six weeks. He had used strychnine only. This was the latest available information.

I had come prepared for a poison campaign. Numerous experiments showed me many things. The wolves were my teachers. Eventually this was the plan I adopted. When killing a beef for ranch use, take the pluck i.e. the heart and lungs together for a drag; make a bag of the fresh rawhide, touch it not at all with the bare hands, and as little as possible with the steel knife. Wear leather gloves rubbed with fresh blood. Do not breathe on it. Enclose two grains of strychnine in a gelatin capsule, cut baits of beef or suet, two by three inches, make a hole in each with a sharp bone, push in the capsule. A pair of wooden pinchers is necessary to lift the baits. Finally, make a drag by fastening the pluck of the beef to your rope which is looped on your saddle horn. This trails on the ground twenty feet behind your horse; and at every quarter-mile or less, you lift a poison bait from the bag and drop it on the trail.

The theory is that a wolf or coyote will strike this trail, and follow it eagerly. Coming to the bait, he will gobble that and still follow; so that he dies on the line, and is easily found. But for that, he might go a quarter-mile to one side and die in a thicket, never to be discovered. With coyotes this worked perfectly well. Many a coyote did I get by means of poison, but never once a gray wolf. Then two incidents happened which gave me plenty of food for thought.

Early one morning I was riding the drag of the day before, when I saw, nearly a quarter mile ahead, a coyote also on my drag. He stopped at something, evidently a poison bait, and devoured it. He went on 200 yards, then fell in the first horrible convulsion of strychnine poisoning. I galloped up and drew my gun to end his suffering. The ball went over his head. However, now he knew his enemy. He staggered to his feet, vomited all he had in his stomach, then sought to escape. He dragged his paralyzed hind legs on the ground, but worked desperately with forefeet, snapping at his own flank and legs with frenzied jaws.

I rode and fired again—and again missed. He made another

desperate effort. I followed fast and far and soon realized that I was making him take the remedy that was the only successful solution: "puke up the poison, get up and fight for your life."

I fired again and again, but gradually his desperate efforts found response in his hind legs. He drove his will power into them—they worked—he went faster and faster; and at length, although I followed for half a mile on a good horse, he gradually faded away in a great stretch of scrubby gullies.

These things I now realized. Had I let him alone, he would have died where first he took the bait. But I made him take the one possible remedy—get up and fight for his life. Next, they would ever after know and fear the smell of strychnine and would teach other coyotes to do the same.

I had often found my poison victims with gashes on loins and on limbs. I knew now that these were self-inflicted in their agony.

The other incident, a never-to-be-forgotten tragedy, took place at a neighboring ranch. It was a cold wet night in late November, frost in the air, wet snow everywhere, when Natty Lincoln rode in about ten o'clock. He was nearly frozen. The resident boys were in bed.

Nat turned his horse loose and walked in. "Say Jack," he called, "have you any quinine? I'm all in."

"Sure," said Jack. "On the shelf back of the stove."

Yes, there it was in the dim light—a fat little bottle, the familiar ounce container of the quinine. Nat took a dipper of water and swallowed a spoonful of the quinine.

"Gosh," he exclaimed, "that's the bitterest quinine I ever tasted."

Then he fell on the ground, writing and screaming in agony. The other boys jumped out of their beds in sudden terror.

"What is it? What's up?"

"Jack, Jack, if ever in my life I done you a kindness, for God's sake, take your gun and kill me! I got the wrong bottle. I got the wolf poison.

Shrieking in agony, poor Nat went down again and in three more minutes was dead.

I was not in that ranch house at the time, but I was in the neighborhood and got the story first-hand from those who were there. It affected me deeply. What right, I asked, has man to inflict such horrible agony on fellow beings, merely because they do a little damage to his material interests? It is not right; it is horrible. I put out no more poison baits.

"Dude Among the Cowboys"

When I began life at Bender's ranch, it was clearly set forth that Bender was to be cook and housekeeper; I was a boarder wholly occupied with wolf hunting. Very soon, however, I found that Bender hated to get up early. My habit was to rise about seven; he would lie abed till nine, unless dragged out.

The difference it made to me was the preparing of breakfast. This third morning, seeing no sign of life from Bender's room, I quickly made my own breakfast about seven. Of course, it was only common decency that I cook enough for two.

The next morning was worse and later. The morning after that I realized I had positively been forced into the office of cook. Bender seemed quite satisfied to let it go at that, and would even lie awake for half an hour, awaiting the summons, "Jim, breakfast."

"Ha, ha!" said I to myself. "This is a situation I have seen handled elsewhere.

Jim was fond of hot biscuit for breakfast. So next morning I rose early, made a nice batch of biscuit for myself, then a special batch for Jim. But I made his with washing soda instead of baking soda. He got up lazily some time after I had finished, bit into a biscuit, exposed its bright yellow bitter, and spat it out, saying, "What in hell is that matter with this biscuit?"

"Is there something the matter?" I asked. "There's the stuff I made them of." I waved by hand toward the cupboard where indeed were all the tins. "Mine were all right."

The next morning, having finished my breakfast, I put a handful of salt in the coffee pot and shouted, "Jim, get up, breakfast."

Jim got up, poured himself a cup of coffee and at once exploded, "Say, Seton, did you make this coffee of slough water, it's strong of alkali."

"Jim, I made that coffee of the very water you brought in last night—you said, from the spring. I know I found it all right. You seem to have a taste in your mouth, a hangover. Have you been drinking?"

Jim struggled through the rest of the breakfast in a very bad humor.

Beefsteak was, of course, our staple food. Next morning, I not only doctored the coffee pot, I fried Jim's portion of steak in axle grease. Poor Jim! He ran out of printables, and his language became most unparliamentary.

"Seems to me, Jim," I said, "you've had an awful hangover the last few days. Now, if you don't like my cooking, you know what you can do.

"Yes, I know. I know it's the law of the range that the feller who kicks on the cooking takes the job. Yes, I know—and I'm *kicking* right now. I ain't going to be pisened by you or your cooking. I don't know how you stood it. I'm cooking after this."

Which he did. I bore it bravely, however, and harbored no grudge against him. And it was twenty years afterward before Jim learned how I made him force my resignation as cook.

This did not mean that I did not help some with the commissary. Jim noticed that I was quite expert cutting the steaks from the quarter of beef that always hung in the shade of the shanty, so he left that job to me.

One day I remarked, "Jim, there's not enough beef left for a week. You don't like it fresh and hot any more than I do. Can't we stock up so it gets properly 'hung'?"

"You bet. We'll corral some this morning."

So, after breakfast, we mounted our horses. The vast open plain was spotted here and there with bunches of cattle. The nearest contained about thirty head of steers and heifers.

We drove these to our corral, but could not get them to enter. It seems that two days before some Mexican shepherds had butchered a sheep, hanging it on the gate to skin. Gate and fence were smeared with blood. This always excites or terrifies cattle; and each time our bunch drew near the gate they recoiled, and stampeded in spite of us.

After half an hour of failure, I said, "It's no use, Jim. Show me which one to take, and I'll drop him in his track."

"Yes, and have him blatting and bleeding all over the plains. Nothing doing."

After another half hour of futile effort, I said, "Show me which one to take, and I guarantee he'll drop where his is."

"Then take the red 'Bar-O'."

I steadied my horse and leveled my rifle. But before I could draw, Jim shouted, "What in hell are you shootin' at?"

"That red steer," I replied.

"No, this heifer," he indicated. I put the rifle ball in the center of the heifer's forehead, and she fell. The rest of the cattle scattered over the plain. The air was full of dust. I feared for the gunlock and went off toward the house.

"Where are you goin'?" shouted Jim.

"To put the gun indoors," I answered.

"Leave that gun here. We may need it," was his answer. I did so, in silence, somewhat puzzled.

Then we set about skinning the heifer. I never saw skinning more hurriedly or more badly done. We chopped off head, feet, and tail, without skinning them, and Jim at once put these out of sight in a mudhole. Then we flayed the carcass, so quickly that chunks of meat were still quivering with life after they were slashed from the body, but yet fast to the hide. We rolled her over to skin the other side where I saw the brand.

"This isn't you brand, is it?" I exclaimed.

His answer was blunt, "It don't do to know too much about brands in New Mexico." So I kept quiet.

We chopped the carcass crudely into about eight pieces, and in four big tin washtubs carried these indoors.

I knew that law required the hide of a new-killed beef to hang on the corral fence for one month, brand displayed. So when Jim hurriedly rolled up to hide and shoved it deep down in a mudhole, I began to think things.

We now made our noon meal, and after it were sitting idling, when far off on the plain I noticed a peculiar flashing. Jim looked, then got up. In this country a flashing like that usually stood for a Mexican rider, the sun on the silver gear on his hat or trappings was characteristic.

The rider drew nearer. Jim went outdoors to meet him. I went into the back room, where the meat in the tubs stood on the floor. Soon, I heard an angry conversation in Mexican. I did not understand it, but disliked the tones.

In the floor of my room was a trapdoor. I opened this and tumbled all the meat out of sight.

On the table was a bouquet of autumn flowers in a water pitcher. I set the table on the trapdoor, sat down near by, got out my sketchbook and began a drawing of those flowers.

The row outside grew louder. Suddenly the door was violently flung open, and in marched a wild-looking Mexican cowman with a revolver in his hand, closely followed by Jim who was unarmed.

I nodded, "Buenos dias," as they came in. The Mexican scowled around the room, then entered the kitchen glared around, went round the house outside, and finally rode away muttering. I thought I saw a look of relief on Jim's face when the coast was clear, but he said nothing. I went on with my flower sketch.

Thirty miles to the south of us, in a small and lonely ranch, dwelt a successful wolf hunter named Tannerey. He had a number of original trapping tricks that he kept to himself; but one day at the "Town Club," he told Jim Bender that he would show me some if I came around some time.

I had been working away using traps and poison every day with limited success. I got a few coyotes right along, but no gray wolves, although there was plenty of proof that they came to my baits and scorned them.

So, one afternoon, after midday meal, I mounted my horse. Jim Bender said, "Where now?"

I replied, "I'm going down to Tannerey to see if I can't learn how to circumvent these wolves."

"Good gosh!" he answered. "You can't go now. You'd get there after dark."

"Well," I answered, "if I don't know the trail, the horse does."

"That ain't it. Ye see Tannerey's an outlaw; there's two warrants out for him. So he always shoots any one comin' near the house after dark. He shot his older brother five months ago."

"Hm," says I, "that's different. I'll wait till morning."

I prepared to make the trip early the next day. As I rode past the door, Jim came to me, made a gesture of "stop," then he did a little courtesy that is usual among cowhands. He bent over and tightened my cinch. Most horses blow up their bellies a little when the saddle goes on, so it is customary to tighten the cinch after ten or fifteen minutes.

Jim looked around, and although there was no one else within ten miles, he made his next remark in a whisper, "I've told Tannerey you are a safe man to have around. You know then to keep your mouth shut. Gosh! I was mighty glad last week when I come in with the crazy greaser and found ye had hid the meat."

On the strength of this recommendation, I was admitted to the Tannerey house that afternoon and saw then and afterward many things I did not wish to see.

I had arrived at the Tannerey ranch before sunset and, therefore, was in no danger of being shot. I had met several of the family before, so needed no introduction. The household consisted of the old father and mother, tall rugged folk that might have hailed from the eastern mountains, the eldest son, the wolver and outlaw, the younger son, a regular cowboy and his young wife.

The house, a log structure, consisted of but one room, with an immense bed on one side, not less than sixteen feet wide, and a cook stove and table at one end. A few chairs completed the furnishing.

I had ridden a bad horse two days back, and that day had covered thirty miles on a rough trail. So, at nine o'clock, I was ready to turn in. I supposed they would bed me for the night in some outhouse, and said, rather timidly,

"Say, boys, if it's all right, I should like to hit the hay."

"Sure, turn in," was the hearty reply, and the eldest son motioned toward the big bed.

"Where?" I asked hesitatingly.

"You better get in there," and the big outlaw pointed to the extreme east. I slipped off most of my clothes and slid under the blanket as modestly as possible. Soon the young wife announced that she also would retire. She took off her outer clothes, slipped under the quilts and there completed disrobing.

One by one, the rest of the family got into this big family bed. When all were in, the arrangement was obviously correct—the old father at the extreme west, then the old mother, next the young wife, the young husband, then the big outlaw brother, and last on the outside, myself—everything perfectly proper and all contingences provided for.

We were up at six in the morning and soon the outlaw proposed a scheme. He had some cattle interests on the Canadian River. It was a good region for gray wolves, so the trip would be of double profit.

He asked, "Which would you rather, ride or drive?" As I was still suffering from my outlaw horse, I said, "Drive."

My legs were badly chafed, my neck was half crippled by the wicked pounding of that black bronco. I had many other sore points as a result of "staying with him," so I really meant it when I said, "Drive."

We loaded the light chuck wagon with our outfit. Then came the usual fight to get the bronco hitched up. It was at length achieved by roping and half killing those two wild beasts.

As soon as I was seated with feet braced forward and reins around my wrists, I said, "Let 'er go."

The two cowmen jerked loose the hog-ties, the broncos sprang to their feet and, of course, ran away. I did not care as long as I could keep the wagon from upsetting and the harness from breaking. The first two miles was a simple runaway. Then my noble steeds were ready to slow down.

"No, no," said I. "You ran away for your pleasure, now you run for mine," and I plied the blacksnake whip. I kept them jumping for five or six miles, when they were willing to take orders and gave not further trouble.

It was blustery when we started but soon grew more so. At sundown we reached the Canadian River. It was bitterly cold—a real norther, a penetrating wind. So we sought out a cut bank with south exposure, protected on north, east, and west.

We lighted our fire, the first I ever made with buffalo chips, and cooked and ate our meal in comparative shelter. Then the two Texans got out their pipes. Alas for me, I never smoked in my life. As we idled the evening away, the big outlaw cut a spike of the Spanish bayonet, smoothed the sand in front of him; then, with the bayonet, made three rows of curious signs. Turning to me, he said, "Jim Bender sez you are kind o' an artist, can take a pencil and make reg'lar pictures jest like printin'. Kin ye make a sign all them signs could be turned into by addin' a few touches?" and in the dust, he pointed out his drawing of the cattle brands of the three great companies in the region.

Having nothing else to do, I worked away at it till I solved the problem by adding a dot here and a bar there. Each of these strange markings could be turned into a curious Arabic inscription which I drew in the dust.

"Say, Billy, ain't that great! Don't forget it," exclaimed the outlaw. And no more was said about it.

We retired soon and slept hard. Early in the morning we sought out a sheltered camp and prepared for a couple of days' stay.

The two men put out a few traps near camp and did it very badly, I thought. Then they took a branding iron from the wagon. As I looked inquiringly, they remarked, "The brands gits haired over; we hev to touch 'em up once in a while, and most of our cattle is down this way."

The cold wind had driven many of the cattle from the north into the sheltered valley. Once or twice that day, I saw the boys in the distance catching cattle, both, of course, were experts with the rope.

Soon their operations were in plain sight. First, a brisk fire of buffalo chips and wood in a deep hole gave them the chance to heat the branding iron. From the nearby herds, they would select some promising animal, preferably a young cow—all the better if the brand on it was somewhat haired over; rope her, and while one held her down by the lasso kept tight, thanks to a well-trained horse, the other wielded the hot iron, and speedily turned the original brand into the one I had unwittingly invented for them. The whole operation took barely twenty minutes for each animal. The new brand could be registered at the county office at later convenience.

These men had added twenty or thirty cattle to their wealth before I was fully aware of their proceedings.

That morning, after they had worked so near camp that I could not be mistaken, I faced them at the nooning, thus,

"Say, boys, I came to New Mexico to do some wolf hunting, not to learn the cattle business. And I'm not going to learn it."

"The hell you ain't," grouched the outlaw. And he drew his gun. "Ain't you into it like the rest of us?"

"No, I am not."

"Didn't you invent that slick counter brand?"

"I didn't know what it was for." He was covering me, and if I had laid my hand on my gun, would have killed me right then and there, for he had a witness. But I kept my hands up.

Then the younger man said, "Say, Tom, he's all right. He'll keep his mouth shut."

"Yes," I said, "I'll keep my mouth shut about your business, and you can do the same about mine. But I am going back today if I have to walk."

The big fellow was very ready to finish me. But the younger man called him aside and whispered something.

Then the outlaw said, "Well, we're out of grub anyway. Guess we'll all start back." Which we did.

The only allusion he made to the subject was just before we parted at the end of the journey.

"Jim Bender says you're O.K., so I suppose ye know enough to keep your mouth shut."

"I do," was my reply. And I did—until now.

Albert W. Thompson

Albert Thompson grew up in Maine but came to Colorado as an eighteen-year-old freshman at Colorado College, Colorado Springs in the fall of 1884. The following year he headed for the open range country of northeastern New Mexico after hearing from friends of substantial profits to be made in the cattle business.

He spent his first winter with a cow outfit on Tramperos Creek where he learned the rudiments handling cattle on the open range.

Early in 1886 he filed on 160 acres under that 1841 Preemption Act on Pinavetitos Creek which is roughly twenty miles from present day Clayton, New Mexico. The following spring he joined the Lake Ranch Cattle Company's roundup which embarked from its headquarters on Ute Creek. The Illinois-based company ran 12,000 head of mother cows on open range and had a remuda of over 200 saddle horses. Thompson worked both the spring roundup that saw more than 2000 calves branded with the company's HT brand and the fall beef roundup when the marketable steers were gathered and driven to the Santa Fe stockyards in Springer where they were shipped to Kansas City for sale. His recollections of those roundups are included here.

In 1889 Thompson was appointed postmaster of the newly created town of Clayton. Four years later he took a position at the United States Land Office registering land claims throughout northeastern New Mexico.

Later in life he wrote about his experiences on the range as a young man for a number of magazines and local newspapers that he compiled into the book, *They Were Open Range Days: Annals of a Western Frontier* (1946).

A W THOMPSON
P. O. Tramperas, Mora Co.

Some Cattle branded ⊽ on left. side Ear-mark
Overhalf crop Each Ear
Increase branded [brand] on left side and 4 on
left hip   Horse [brand] brand 4 on left hip
Range on head of [brand] Tramperas

Albert W. Thompson's brand registered in 1886.

132

They Were Open Range Days: Annals of a Western Frontier
Denver: World Press Company, 1946

"Great Roundups Were in Order Then"

The Lake Ranch Cattle Company, usually called from its brand "the HT outfit" -- top of T over left top of H—was a Peoria, Illinois, corporation. Its headquarters in 1887 occupied a draw in which several copious springs trickled from the base of a gravel-strewn ridge, 200 yards from Ute Creek.

Its site was treeless. Improvements consisted of a long adobe and stone building, dirt roof, of three rooms, which served as camp house and kitchen for the hands. Behind it, stables and corrals. Twenty yards south stood the boss's headquarters—office and sleeping room. The HT was not one of the largest cattle companies in northeastern New Mexico. In 1887, it probably owned 12,000 cattle. In 1883, it branded 2,000 calves. Its stockholders, in 1884, were offered $350,000 by a Kansas City Commission firm for their lands, cattle and horses, which they unwisely declined. A dozen years later, with cows selling for $10, the HTs sold out and took their losses.

The HT remuda in 1887 consisted of 200 cow horses. Some were gentle, others refractory—"buckers." I recall one of the latter which I rode that summer, "Little Billy," a chunky dun, who took his daily morning exercises out on me. These consisted of wild evolutions and contortions, always followed by an empty saddle. Before the season closed, Billy and I got along better.

Jeff Towner, top cowman and HT's range manager, was slow-spoken, dignified, urbane. He possessed the indefinable art of governing men. I can see him now, as on "Percy," his large, gray, sagacious "cut horse," he moved slowly and without bustle when cutting out cattle from the roundup. Jeff and Percy played the game with almost Centaur precision. When Percy discovered just what animal Jeff wanted to cut out, the feat was as good as performed.

The HT was to furnish me with ten cowhorses. I was to receive no wages, but board at a roundup wagon was always free of cost to a worker. Tent, camp bed, saddle and bridle I supplied.

Our complement of men during the round-up season of 1887 numbered, with those from other ranches who worked with us, ten or twelve, besides horse rustler and cook. All preparations having been made for our departure from the ranch on the 26th of May we climbed into our saddles and, following the chuck wagon, started for the red-dyed Canadian River 75 miles south where we expected to join other outfits in what was known as the "spring hunt."

Suppose we glance at some of the features of northeastern New Mexico's leading industry 60 (1946) years ago, when cattle were left to wander and drift across miles of open expanse, to be followed and returned to home ranges but twice each year, and the machinery and devices employed in carrying out this portion of the business—the round-up.

By general consent, a rancher must own land bordering a stream at which his stock could obtain water and to turn stock loose on the open range without first securing a ranch location and one with water thereon was considered unethical, and a person attempting to do so was sure to meet anything but a cordial reception. This unwritten law of the range was seldom violated. To be sure, the ranchman's cattle were very rarely found near his home, except just after the round-up season in summer when they had been gathered and driven thither. To illustrate the miles of separation existing between the ranchman and his stock, John C. Hill of Clayton told me that in the spring roundup of 1880 when he was working on this range (the roundup started work at Adobe Walls on the Canadian River), he found a Triangle Dot cow belonging to the Dorsey ranch near Springer. She had wandered not less than 180 miles from home but was retaken and driven back.

It was an interesting sight, the array of roundup wagons, summer home of the cowboys, as they congregated preparatory to, and actually engaged in, the work of collecting stock and branding calves. In the summer of 1887, I recall counting 22 roundup wagons camped at the mouth of Leon near Clapham, each wagon having a complement of 150 saddle horses and from ten to fifteen cowboys, besides cook and horse wrangler, the latter's duties confined solely to the custody of the saddle bunch during the day time. This place was the meeting ground of the lower or Canadian River roundup and the western owners from about Raton to Springer.

The early morning maneuvers were novel and picturesque as cowboys saddle up for the "swing" with bucking horses, much confusion, a mingling of savage yells and violent profanity as a man was sent skyward from an ungovernable pony, which, freed of its rider, dashed prairieward, pursued by a dozen "waddies" (cowboys) all throwing ropes and apparently endeavoring to frighten the now dazed animal into further irresponsibility, a situation which will long be remembered by those witnessing this phase of western life.

Often the cowboys were obliged to ride 15 miles from the proposed round-up place before starting to bring in the cattle, and the "swing" from the location I am describing here at the junction of the Leon and Pinavetitos, extended nearly to the Texas line. The story of the roundup, which took place here each year for many seasons, is something as follows:

About the first of May, the large cattle companies, having engaged their men, usually for a period of six months or so—for the cowboy, unless of unusual attainments, was not employed during the winter months—gathered up their "cow horses," which for the winter months had been turned into the small protected horse pasture to hustle for themselves, got their wagon supplies from the railway, and all being in readiness for the summer work, moved south toward the Canadian River which was the point where the first spring roundup was to be made. This spot on the Canadian was at Red River Springs some ten miles down stream from the present town of Logan on the Rock Island Railway. For some days after arrival, the outfits camped here, resting and grazing the saddle horses, awaiting the coming of all the expected roundup wagons and men. During those first days, there was very little to do—guarding the horses at night, and lying in the welcome shade of a wagon sheet suspended at the rear of the chuck wagon by day, or visiting neighboring outfits camped a mile or so apart. The journey from the ranch had been slowly accomplished, moving on ten or fifteen miles each day.

The roundup or chuck wagon was an amazing creation. It

contained the needs—and much of the worldly goods—of the dozen or more men who went along with it for a two months' absence from the ranch. Usually a large wagon, often a "Shuttler," was used. At the rear end of this was the chuck box, an upright cabinet with its front on hinges which, when let down, formed a table supported by two legs attached thereto. On top of the chuck box was the pot rack in which all the sheet-iron kettles and generous coffee pot were carried, while beneath was the potbox, where Dutch ovens found places. Within this chuck box were compartments and drawers for the reception of bread, plates, cups, knives, forks and spoons. One drawer was reserved for the exclusive use of the wagon boss. In this were kept his papers, brand book, and other chattels he desired to take along with him.

Compartments, too, for cans holding sugar and syrup for the daily needs of the men were also in evidence, and often other ingenious devices for the use of all concerned were observed. On one side of the wagon between the wheels the water barrel was held in place and kept filled with water for the cook and the members of the wagon crew for drinking purposes. Often camping places were made near some surface water which, though it could be used when cooking, was unfit for drinking.

Within the wagon were flour, grain for the mules which moved us from camp to camp, camp beds, rope for lariats and staking purposes, wood for the cook's use, canned tomatoes, canned corn and dried fruit. On the side of the chuck box was fastened a mirror before which the cowboy performed his brief toilet, combing his hair and drying his face and hands on the one towel which answered for a dozen men. Sanitation and germs were theories then undiscovered. Nobody suffered.

To return to our camp on the Canadian River which was established about June 5. After several days with little to occupy us, the appointed hour for roundup work to begin arrived. The past days had been spent in various ways by the boys. Some attended to the necessity of washing clothes, the nearest laundry being inconveniently 100 miles away. It was expected that the cow hands should gather wood, fuel for the cook's use. If the Canadian was bank-full, which often happened about the middle of May, the punchers vied with one another and with those of other wagons, in swimming the turbulent stream on their horses, a dangerous though exciting pastime. Sometimes both rider and his horse were drowned. I cannot recall that the wagon bosses used much restraint in this practice. Once a cowboy's horses had been assigned to him, they were his to use as he chose until the end of the season. Each man, as I have stated, had from nine to twelve horses, one of which was for night use while his rider was on night guard, the animal being allowed to graze during the day. This horse was gentle and accustomed to the rope with which he was tethered near the chuck wagon ready for the two-hour circle around the cattle bedded, perhaps, a mile from the camp. The cowboy also, and more particularly the wagon bosses, had one or two horses used only for "cutting" out cattle from the roundups. Once finding the cow or steer that the rider wished to remove therefrom, these well-trained animals would follow it to the edge of the herd, dodging back and forth until the animal was deposited outside within the proper bunch.

Amid much confusion, this first day of the actual work of rounding up began. The horses were brought into the camp early in the morning and held in a circle by the cow hand who had been guarding them through the night. When the animals had quieted down sufficiently, work of catching one the rider desired began by throwing a lariat over its head. In a few minutes, a dozen of the strugglers were dragged forth and saddling commenced. The strongest horses, those of greatest endurance, were selected for the first circle; many of these were the most refractory in the cavyard.

Headed by the wagon boss, the members of the outfit now sought the starting point for the first circle and, after an absence of two or three hours, returned driving with them all the cattle found. These made a number of bunches which were called the "roundup." After the men had changed horses, cutting out commenced. Stock belonging to the company or to outside men with it, was removed from a bunch and, this done, from another bunch until after all the brands were thoroughly inspected, the rest of the cattle were turned loose. Then there was a mad ride for dinner at the wagon which had moved up near the roundup grounds while the men were out on circle. After dinner, the branding of calves began, the wagon boss doing the roping on his "rope horse" and the men on foot flanking the young creatures as they were drawn close to a fire in which branding irons were heated. Branding was hard work and consumed, not infrequently, most of the afternoon. The cattle which were held were known as the day herd and were grazed during the day and guarded at night until the range of their owners was reached.

The branding finished, some little time was enjoyed by the men in rest before supper. Tents were pitched—usually of the eight by eight "teepee" pattern, beds spread out within them and other necessary work performed. Supper was served about five o'clock and the welcome yell of "Chuck," accompanied by the beating on a tin plate by the cook was received with much gusto, for appetites in cow camps were always keen. Some of the range chefs had unique announcements when meals were ready. One was, "Here is hell—come and get it," and other sobriquets, the meanings of which were never mistaken.

Here I wish to pay my compliments to Albert Stuff who, in the summer of 1887, was the HT chuck-wagon cook, where for seven or more months I was a member. Bread was baked in Dutch ovens and meat fried in this same kind of vessel. I have seen a shower falling in the afternoon when it became necessary for us to hold slickers over the wood fire or, if far off on the prairie, of "bull chips," when it seemed all but impossible to get a meal ready; yet we always had a good meal. Great expedience was exercised. Bread made from sour dough was baked in these ovens—and such biscuits, perhaps six inches tall, light and sweet, I have rarely eaten.

For breakfast we had fried beef (a yearling was usually selected as best and tenderest for immediate use which, after being roped in the herd, was killed and dressed), bread, coffee, and stewed fruit. Dinner gave us soup, roast beef, shortribs and potatoes, canned corn or tomatoes, apricots, prunes or apples, and some sort of pudding—rice or bread— and for supper again fried beef or boiled beef, bread, and fruit. The cooks rarely had canned milk though one chuck wagon chef boasted that his management gave him everything he wanted, even "dense" milk and "distracted" lemon.

Stuff, our cook, before we left the ranch in May, 1887, packed in several five-gallon empty oilcans, as many eggs as he could, which later were used in cakes, sometimes with a filling made from canned tomatoes. Evening finally closed the long day. After supper, the first of four guards, standing two hours turn, took charge of the cattle which usually became quiet as they were gently drawn into a circle and by midnight most of them had bedded down, a few, however, standing as sentinels. The two men on guard rode in opposite directions about the herd, meeting twice in completing the trip, thus giving the animals little opportunity to escape.

The punchers in night riding were likely to be musically inclined and, while often the stumbling of a horse or a jack rabbit jumping up near the herd would stampede the whole bunch, stock bore with amazing patience the weird incantations to which the cowboy sometimes gave voice. Some of the songs rehearsed in the long night hours I recall in part. They were usually doleful. One popular song began...

"I am a roving cowboy from off the western plains,
I ride the festive bronco and draw the saddle reins"

...to which were a dozen stanzas. We had puncher with us in the summer of 1887 from Texas, who had an apparently inexhaustible collection of high-proof cowboy ditties, as original as were the chantyman's refrains of clipper ship days, which he sang when on day herd as well as in the night.

On night guard, if the cattle were quiet, the riders would occasionally halt and converse briefly as they met. We watched, too, the Great Dipper as it slowly revolved around the North Star and picked out other constellations—for the New Mexico nights were usually clear and cloudless. Then came time to call the next guard, which one man did, while his companion stayed with the herd. No man will fail to recall, as he lay in his camp bed perhaps fast asleep, the sound of an incoming rider approaching camp, dismounting with jingling spurs, pulling apart the tent flap and announcing quietly, so he might not disturb other sleepers, "Third guard," and of the quick action of the called in getting out onto his horse and off to the cattle to which, even in the blackest night, the well-trained animal bore him. Nor will he forget, with a big herd to handle, how all hands went off into the gloom and rain in front of the restless kine which attempted to crowd by him. Wet to the skin, he sat in the saddle until dawn found him miles from camp but his charges safe.

Among the more or less valuable possessions of the author is a small, worn diary bearing the date of the year 1887, which he carried that summer on the roundup. Excerpts from this little book will serve as a guide to the itinerary of our chuck wagon and its daily work.

Leaving the ranch on May 18, 1887, by slow stages we reached a site close to the junction of Ute Creek and Canadian where we were in camp awaiting the coming of the roundup which was working up the former stream. "With us here is an AL wagon," my diary states. Finally, on Wednesday, June 8, the cavalcade of wagons, men, and horses—with them the thousands of cattle which had been collected on the heated prairies below—reaching us, we joined them in actual work. On June 10, we had moved up Ute Creek to Rincon Colorado—then the Gallegos Ranch—on the 12th to a camping spot just below the Bar T Cross Ranch, on the 15th moving across from the Tequesquite to Ute Creek—again near the Baca Ranch in "much rain and mud," finally ending up on the 19th at the HT Ranch where the herd, which had thus far been collected, was turned loose. Then, immediately off on another "hunt," this time moving to the mouth of the Leon some 35 miles from the ranch where the great aggregation of outfits assemble annually, of which I have before made mention.

Up the Leon, across to the Pinvetitos to be on the Foster Ranch by June 24, and so on to the head of the Tramperos; then to Upper Ute Creek and to the ranch to turn loose the cattle we had found. Enumeration of this daily life may not be of further interest. It ended after several short periods of rest during the summer and fall, on November 4th at Springer, when the "beef" herd—the steers of the company—were corralled and, cars having been ordered, these were shipped to Kansas City to be sold.

Pleasantly the memory of the last night I stood guard about these thousand or more three and four-year-old steers, in company with one other member of the outfit, of the clear cold of that early morning—we had been out in one or two snowstorms in late October—of the herd which, unmindful of its fate of shipment and sale, was bedded contentedly near the Springer stockyards, for this was the nearest shipping point—and a famous one, to be superseded by Clayton 100 miles distant two or three years later on the building of the Fort Worth & Denver City Railroad—vividly these last days of the roundup of that year come to mind, the return of the chuck wagon to the ranch, a distance of 60 miles, and of my parting with the excellent fellows and with Stuff, the cook, which immediately followed.

Perhaps in no less manner did the worker on the range form a deep regard for the horses he had ridden and to whose companionship he had become affectionately attached. I recall, after all these years, most of the names of the ten fine animals that composed my mount that year, of "O Z," my night horse which, as I have testified always knew the way to the herd and was seemingly aware when our two hours were up and anxious to go to camp to call the next guard—who never became bewildered no matter how dark the night nor stormy the weather. "O Z" was a well-trained veteran.

With the incoming tide of colonization, passed into memory only, the free-range cattle raising industry of northeastern New Mexico. It was magnificent in its conception and operation and, for some years, profitable. Its height was reached about 1884 and its gradual decadence and end occurred a few years later. One by one the great cattle companies sold livestock and lands and the vast area in which they conducted business, finally unopposed by them, was taken up by smaller men—and the great herds disappeared forever.

N. Howard (Jack) Thorp

N. Howard (Jack) Thorp

Jack Thorp was born into an affluent New York City family in 1867 but spent his growing up years working summers on his brother's ranch in Nebraska. Enamored by cowboy life, he went to New Mexico in 1886 to punch cows on the vast Bar W Ranch outside of Carrizozo in the Tularosa Basin of Lincoln County.

While riding for the Bar Ws, he became interested in the songs that cowboys sang while on night herd and around the fire in camp at night. In the spring of 1889, he decided to collect as many range ballads as he could and embarked on a journey with "a good saddle and pack horse and a few dollars in my pockets" to visit cow outfits in New Mexico and Texas. He wrote down the words to songs the cowboys sang, often while riding with them horseback. When his trip was over, he bought two hundred longhorn cows and starting ranching in the San Andres Mountains using the Slash SW brand.

In 1908 he compiled twenty-three of the songs he had collected on his travels into a pamphlet he titled, "Songs of the Cowboys," that was published in Estancia, New Mexico. One of the songs included was "Little Joe the Wrangler" that he wrote on a cow drive from Chimney Lake, New Mexico to Higgins, Texas in 1898. It continues to be one of the most popular cowboy songs ever written and is still frequently performed.

In 1926 he published a collection of stories about his time on the New Mexico range in a book titled, *Tales of the Chuckwagon*. In the late 1930s he worked for the New Mexico Federal Writers' Program writing about his experiences and collecting stories and songs from former cowpunchers he knew. He also published stories in *New Mexico*

Magazine, *The Cattleman*, *The Atlantic Monthly*, and *The Literary Digest* among others.

After Thorp died in Alameda, New Mexico in June, 1940, his long-time friend Neil Clark compiled many of his stories, both published and in manuscript form, into the book, *Pardner of the Wind* (1941). The excerpts that follow are from that book and include Thorp's reminiscences of some of his favorite horses and a description of a typical New Mexico spring roundup. The stories about his horses demonstrate what James Hinkle, governor of New Mexico and former top hand on the Pecos River, once wrote, "What time cowboys were not rolling cigarettes or talking branding, they were bragging about their pet horses."

Pardner of the Wind
Caldwell, ID: The Caxton Printers, Ltd., 1941

"Spanish Thunderbolts"

The story of the cow horse has been over romanticized but little understood. It is one of the great chapters in the history of the West. The range cattle industry never could have existed without those small Spanish thunderbolts that turned on a dime and flashed into top speed at the flick of a spur, the progeny of Arabians brought over by the Conquistadors. A modern cowboy hauls his horse in a trailer behind his flivver till he gets to where the road ends. The old time cowboy never saw a steering wheel. He was given a mount, usually seven horses, when he went to work for an outfit. They were his as long as he kept the job. He trained them himself and was jealous of anybody else riding them. A ranch owner once told cowboy Pete Sommers that he had a great friend coming out from the East, and he wanted Pete's old Rusty horse for him to ride.

"Sure, cut him out." Pete's words were like icicles on the bunkhouse roof in a long cold winter. "While you're at it, cut out the whole mount and make out my paycheck."

A real cowhand wouldn't let anybody else ride his horses. No two men handle a horse alike, and a cow horse and his rider had to understand one another like a bean understands the pod it grows in. Some horses had natural cow sense and took right to it; others never would have any cow sense, no matter how much you trained them.

Cowboys had four main jobs for horses; roping, cutting, riding circle, and standing night guard. Almost any horse with a lot of "bottom" and endurance, but not especially good at anything else would do for

145

riding circle. The last man dropped might be fifteen miles from the wagon before he started hazin' cattle out of the brush and draws, and by the time he drove his gather back to the holding ground, he would have done a lot of riding. It took a good strong horse. For the other jobs, cowboys trained specialists.

A top cutting horse was a second set of brains at the round up. If you started after a certain critter in the herd, and your horse once identified the animal you were after, you could reach over and take the bridle off, and he'd take that particular critter out of the herd by himself. He had to have lots of speed, but he never used it till he had slowly worked the animal out of the herd. In the movies you sometimes see a man supposedly cutting cattle out of the herd, scattering the cattle in all directions which shows that that cowboy or his director knew nothing about the handling of cattle. A cutting horse didn't get to be a top animal without a lot of training, and the best cutting horses were the cowboy's pride.

A top roping horse went into high from the first hop. He watched your rope and stopped the instant he saw you had made your catch. As you ran to make your tie of the animal's legs, he kept a strain on the rope so the animal could not get up. There were no branding chutes in the early days, and all cattle, big or little, were roped and stretched out either in corrals or on the open range. When a big steer or a cow or a bull was roped, the roping horse kept his head to the animal and the rope tight, not only because that was what he was taught to do, but also because anything else was likely to result in his getting snarled up in the rope and thrown. The strain came just behind the horse's shoulders, and at this point he was apt to get tender and sore. Also, holding heavy cattle was hard on the front legs. Some old rope horses were just cute enough to be mighty careful not to run within roping distance of a heavy animal. I once knew two horses that grew up together and were pals, and in their prime they were top roping horses. But as they got older, while they would always make a great show of willingness to overtake a steer, they would never carry the rider quite close enough for a throw.

One spring come roundup time, these two old timers were not to be found at all. Don't tell me they didn't know! For within a week after the crew left for the lower end of the range and the roundup, the two old bums showed up all right at the home watering. The same thing happened the two following years, and the head man told the foreman to let them have their liberty for they had earned it. Both were more than eighteen years old.

You would never see a horse that was tops at both roping and cutting. Plenty cowboys would brag that they owned such horses, but I never saw one, and to expect a horse to be expert at both jobs would be a little like expecting a man to be a great physician and also a great lawyer. A horse seldom became a top horse at either roping or cutting until he was around eight years old. It took that long to learn the tricks. But once he had them learned, he might keep on at the work till he was twenty. Cow horses wore out much more slowly than Eastern horses. The feet of the latter would usually be the first thing to give out due to their being always shod and pounding along hard roads and working every day except possibly Sundays and holidays. A cow horse in a seven horse mount got a half day of work every three days for seven months of the year—thus he had five months of absolute rest. A cutting horse working a herd would usually work only for two or three hours, then he would be pulled out and replaced.

A top night horse had to be gentle and very sure footed in order to protect himself and his rider from falling, and he had to have a good sense for location. Chopo, another pet horse of mine, was the best night horse I ever had. Coal black and branded O, he was one of those horses that made a good hand anywhere. If he made up his mind to catch a calf, he'd catch him, but he was not a top at it. I have even used him in a buggy team. Everything was all right with Chopo. A girl school teacher said once,

"Do you know what that little black horse of yours will do?"

"What?"

"He'll eat peppermint candy. I fed him two long sticks."

I don't think you could feed Chopo anything but what he'd eat it. He saved my life not once, but many times. Chopo's daddy was a Morgan stud shipped out from the East, and his mammy a sure enough mustang Arabian, one of the old Spanish stock that ran pretty much all over the Southwest. He first proved himself on the trail drive when Little Joe the wrangler was killed but not in the same stampede however.

We had just crossed the Pecos. It was one of those black nights, so dark you could feel it. Rain began during the first guard and increased till it was just sloshing down. Lightning striking here and there, seemed to rip the skies apart. In the bright glare we could see that the cattle were on their feet. The rain suddenly turned to hail though it was still warm. Some of the hailstones were half the size of hens' eggs. When a bolt of lightning finally struck at the edge of the herd, twenty-five hundred head of beef steers left the bed ground with a roar like thunder.

Directions are hard to keep at night with no stars out, but as near as I could tell, I was north of the herd when the run started. I aimed to keep to the north and west, matching strides with the leaders, shooting my six gun in front of their noses in an effort to make them turn and mill, and trusting to Chopo to keep his feet. Every once in a while, he broke through the muddy ground, but he never fell. Had he done so, I would have been a mincemeat cowboy in ten seconds under hundreds of hooves. Occasionally a streak of lightning would show me where a steer had fallen and those following had piled up on him.

We were wholly unable to stop the cattle. They ran for miles without a sign of a split. Then when the split did come, it was so dark that I didn't know it till a flash of lightning showed I was riding in the lead of exactly three steers. Of course, it was no use going on. I was soaked to the skin. I had used my slicker trying to whip the steers back and make them mill, and there was nothing much left of it except the sleeves and collar. The air had turned freezing cold. I knew that every hand at the wagon would have been out to try to turn the cattle, but where the others were, and where the wagon was, I hadn't the slightest notion. Neither Chopo nor I had ever been in that particular section before.

Once more it was a case of trust the horse. I gave the little black his head. Hours passed, and I never heard sound or saw sign of another horse or human being. Then suddenly in the distance I thought I saw a spark of light. Another minute and I was sure. Chopo nickered. A horse answered. Chopo not only had made the run without once falling, but also he had brought me straight to the wagon on a night black enough to render human senses absolutely useless.

> *Through rocky arroyos so dark and so deep;*
> *Down the sides of the mountains so slippery and steep;*
> *You're good judgment, sure-footed, wherever you go*
> *You're a safety conveyance, my little Chopo.*

Cowboys were very various in their treatment of horses. Some had no patience and were mean and short tempered, and you could depend on it that a horse of any spirit would give that kind of rider as good as it got. In fact, you could often tell a good deal about the kind of man a puncher was just by noticing how the horse acted when the rider came near. Many cowboys had respect and often affection for their horses, and got a good deal of amusement and education out of studying their ways.

In many respects horses resemble humans. Oddly enough, they seem to have about the same reaction to alcohol as human beings. I had a little pet horse that got to drinking water out of a bottle. One day somebody tried him on whiskey, and he got cockeyed.

I had a horse named Grampa that would steal anything. If you dropped your pocketknife, he'd pick it up. He was a regular old pot licker. At a wagon camp he would watch till he thought everyone was asleep, then he'd sneak close taking little noiseless steps in his hobbles. Many a time I pretended to be asleep in my blankets just to watch him. Unless stopped, he would nose the cover off the cook pot and eat the contents, whether it was beans, coffee, stew, or raw dough. Once at my Slash SW Ranch in the San Andres Mountains, I dropped a bottle of whiskey in the wash bowl on the gallery while I went to the corral for something. Although I returned in a very few minutes, the whiskey was gone, and Grampa was drunker than a dime store mirror.

Range horses had personal likes, dislikes, and prejudices just as human beings do. At one time I was cattle buyer for the San Cristobal Ranch and was on the go pretty much all the time, trading mostly with Indians and small native ranchmen within a distance of seventy-five or a hundred miles. My only assistant was a collie pup named Bobbie Burns, who in time developed into one of the smartest cow dogs I have ever known. My horse was named Clay, a genuine old line-back buckskin that in the past had had the reputation of being a bucking fool but with me was as gentle as one could wish.

On long trips Bobbie Burns would get tired, and I would let him ride in the moral or nosebag which hung on the horn of the saddle. There he would sit with his paws hanging over the sides, looking at the jack rabbits and other scenery. When he got too big for that, he would have to take it mostly afoot. During this time, Clay became very attached to the dog, and whenever I saw that Bobbie was getting too tired, I would stop, reach over, and pull him up by his collar and lay him across in front of me on the saddle. Clay never objected. In fact dog and horse got so accustomed to this act, that when I called Bobbie, he would run and jump as high as he could, landing against the horse's shoulder, and I would grab him and scramble him into the saddle. When full grown, he could make it onto the horse's back without assistance. The dog and horse were thrown together in this way for about two years with no other companions to speak of, and that no doubt accounts for the great fondness that grew up between them. When Clay was turned into a small pasture occasionally for a day's rest, the two would remain together, Clay sometimes whinnying to call the dog to him. Often Bobbie would jump on his back and sit there while the horse continued to graze, both seemingly perfectly happy.

Another horse that knew what he liked was Old Speck, a red roan with a switch tail, no beauty, but all horse. I brought him as a three-year-old from Devil's River, Texas. He was naturally gentle and never had to be broken and adapted himself to any place I wanted to use him, saddle or buggy. He was six years old when I was married, and since he seemed like such a good horse, I gave him to my wife with a new side saddle as a wedding present. Sometime later a fine shorthorn bull of mine strayed to Canyon Blanco, some thirty miles away, and I suggested to my wife that she go along and help me drive him home. We made the trip out by road and had no trouble. We spent some time watching a celebration of a native matachine dance, after which we started back toward the ranch with the bull. The country in that section is heavily timbered mostly with cedar and piñon and a few small pines on the ridges. As soon as we climbed out of the canyon we were among the trees. My wife was riding Speck at the right of the bull. Presently she called to me, and I saw that she was having trouble. Old Speck was trying to brush her off the saddle under a piñon tree. I got them straightened out, but we had not gone far before Speck tried to repeat the performance. This idea, in fact, became so fixed in his mind that it resolved itself into a game. Every inviting looking limb he saw, he would head for. Finally, he became so insistent that she and I had to change horses. Why Speck didn't want my wife to ride him was a mystery to me for she weighed only about half as much as I did. Whenever she tried to ride him after that, he went through the same stunt.

I thought perhaps he merely objected to a woman rider. But that was not the case. A young schoolteacher who was staying for the winter at the ranch could ride Speck and with her aboard he behaved himself perfectly. The only explanation I ever hit on that seemed to made sense was that my wife was a brunette and the schoolteacher a blond and old Speck was a gentleman! If horses could talk, they might be able to tell us just how smart they are, as some humans do!

The worst scare I ever had was given me by a pet horse named Fiddle. I was riding alone, trying to catch up with the chuck wagon, the remuda, and the rest of the outfit, which got half a day's start of me out of Deming. We were bound for the Palomas Lake south of the border in Old Mexico. Forty miles below Deming, after covering some of the lonesomest country I know of with only a couple of windmills in sight along the trail to indicate human beings and the bleak Tres Hermanos Mountains over to the east, I reached the Boca Grande which marks the line between Old and New Mexico. The Boca Grande is only a little river, but it is always running, and there are several little falls in it, not high, but just big enough to make the water noisy. That's where the river got its name; boca grande, big voice. I was unarmed on this trip except for my six-shooter. I carried a slicker, more for style than anything else, as it seldom rains in that country. Since I knew I would have to lay out, I had had some sandwiches put up for myself and a morral full of grain for my horse.

The night before I started, word had reached Deming that bandidos had killed and robbed a couple of freighters at the crossing of the Boca Grande and left the bodies lying in the road. I reached the stream about sunset and before arriving could make out the freighter's wagons ahead. When I got up close I saw how the loads had been ransacked, boxes broken open, and their contents scattered. The bodies of the two men were still sprawled on the ground beside their wagons. From the horse sign, I figured that there had been four or five of the bandits. I didn't know but they might still be in the vicinity.

About half a mile to the west of the wagons was a mesquite thicket. Picking up a couple of cans of tomatoes which had been overlooked in the looting of the boxes, I moseyed over to the thicket, removed Fiddle's saddle and bridle, and with only a rope around his neck, led him the short distance to the Boca Grande to water him. Fiddle was one of those horses that just broke out gentle. He never had a mean idea, wouldn't even run, and just trotted off gentle under his first saddle. With a half hitch around his nose, you could jump on him bareback and ride him anywhere.

Back in camp, I hung the morral with the corn on Fiddle's head, ate my sandwiches, and rolled me a cigarette. Not wishing to attract attention, I decided not to make a fire and kept my eye open for any riders. As soon as Fiddle had finished what I thought was about half of the corn, I took the moral away from him, meaning to save the rest for his breakfast. I hid it from him by placing it under my saddle which had been turned upside down to serve as my pillow. I had two saddle blankets with me, and spreading my leather chaps on the ground, I put one blanket over them and used the other blanket and the slicker for cover.

The sun had been down close to an hour when I noticed Fiddle looking over toward the east. He didn't nicker, just stood and watched. At last I made out what he saw—two riders skylighted away to the east. They didn't worry me much for they weren't headed my way, but I suppose they did sort of color my thoughts.

I pulled off my boots and rolled into bed with my six-shooter in my hand under the covers and between my legs. I was soon dreaming of bandidos and such, and the next thing I knew, something struck me sharply and suddenly in the face. One jump, and I was out of bed and on my feet with my gun jammed against the outlaw's belly. But it was only my little horse, Fiddle.

The rascal had hobbled into camp, nosed out the morral of corn from under the saddle, grabbed it by the bottom with his teeth, and spilled the corn in my face. He had figured it must be time for breakfast.

"Calendar of the Herd"

"Come on, boys, let's go!" the wagon boss called. It was just beginning to get light, and twenty of us set off at a high lope from the wagon. The cook had routed us out of our bedrolls half an hour before, and we had downed a hasty, sleepy breakfast and were off to a day's hard riding grind. The calf roundup, first important event in the calendar of the herd, was getting under way. On this roundup, as in fact on any spring roundup, it was usual to start at the extreme southern end of the range, the wagon camping at the last watering and staying there maybe two or three days until that part of the country was cleaned up of all the cattle which watered there.

All of the cowhands rode out to the rim of a big circle with the wagon roughly somewhere near the center, and from there we started driving in anything on four legs that we found heading for the wagon. The foreman would distribute the men, usually in pairs, assigning them to the different areas—two men, say, to the cottonwood watering, to start everything hightailing towards the wagon, two more to Box Canyon, another two to the Work Mound Springs, three or four to clean out the foothills and watering near Salt Creek, two to Mound Springs, two to Star Springs, and so on. The size of the big circle was determined partly by the nature of the country and partly by the number of men present to work it. Riding circle took a horse with plenty of bottom for in the course of a day's work he was sure to cover a lot of miles. On the out trip, it was the smart thing to save your horse, maybe loping awhile, jog-trotting a few miles, and walking some in order to have him in good shape when you actually started hazing animals out of the brush or the canyons and headed them towards the wagon. You did plenty of riding then and gave your horse plenty of work. Sometimes in a rough terrain, it practically took a crazy man and a race horse to turn the critters and keep them turned.

Now if you happened to be at the chuck wagon watching the roundup, you would soon begin to see clouds of dust rising in all directions on the big circle as the cattle started out of the hills from different quarters towards the flats. Presently some of the bunches began meeting. Whenever a couple of bulls met, they usually had a great time horning and pushing one another around, while the other cattle bellowed and seemed to cheer them on. As the sun got higher and hundreds of cattle had struck the flats, the dust cloud got bigger and thicker and came nearer to the wagon. The first two men out would usually be the first two in, and they would hold their cattle near camp and get them contentedly grazing. This bunch would be added to as the other cattle appeared from the drive. When all were gathered, they would be held under herd that night and calf branding would begin.

Most of the principal waterings had large corrals for the branding, and the procedure was to cut off a small bunch of cattle from those under herd and corral them. A fire was built to heat the branding irons with two men tending it. With them at the fire were two punchers to do the bulldogging or flanking—that is, to throw the calves on their sides and hog-tie their four feet together. Also at the fire was a tally man who kept a record of all the calves branded. Two men on horseback would ride through the cattle in the corral and with little dog loop (small size loops in their ropes) would catch and drag the calves up to the fire for the branding. Each calf, of course, was given the same brand as its mother. If there were any doubt about the ownership, the mother cow would be sorted out of the herd and driven up to the calf to see if she would own it. Generally this was not necessary as the mother cow was likely to follow her calf and be full of business when it was dragged bawling up to the branding fire—in fact, quite often she would go on the prod and keep the punchers dodging to stay out her way.

As soon as every critter picked up in the roundup at that camp was branded, all cattle belonging on the home range were cut out and turned loose. They were shoved in the opposite direction from the roundup's direction of travel so that they would not be picked up again on the next day's drive. The strays were held under herd.

The wagon boss would designate where the next night's camp was to be. At daylight he would start off the cook with the chuck wagon, the wrangler with the remuda, and as many men as necessary with the stray cattle. He would spread the rest of the riders out, fanlike, in a big half circle for a distance of perhaps fifteen miles on each side of the just abandoned camp, with orders to hold everything and drive it in that evening to the next camp which would usually be about ten miles ahead.

This procedure would be continued for a month or six weeks, depending on the size of the range, the branding proceeding daily, and the stray herd increasing in size till the home ranch was reached. Here the strays were held under day herd but were corralled at night to avoid the disagreeable duty of standing night guard.

The next job was to sort (cut) out the different brands of strays. One man was assigned to hold the cut of a given brand as it accumulated, most of the other hands holding the main herd. The stray man representing the brand that had the most critters in the herd would ride in and commence cutting. He would see a cow and calf in his brand. Slowly and with great patience he would work them towards the edge of the herd, then he jumped his horse after them, one of the hands usually giving them a scare, and he hazed them towards the spot where the cut herd was being held. Then he immediately went back for another cow and calf. Cutting was hard, wearying work, keeping man and horse constantly on the alert, and the man doing the cutting would be relieved occasionally while he changed horses. Quite often some bull-headed animal, after being headed for the cut, would whirl around and dash back to the main herd. Then the work had to be done all over. If the same critter tried it again, some puncher would probably "forefoot" him, that is, rope his front feet and throw him so hard that he would be half stunned and would listen to reason. This was called "busting" him.

After the first man to enter the stray herd had trimmed it, that is, cut out everything in his brand that he could find, the roundup boss would ride through the herd to see if he could find a head or two that the other man might have missed. If he found nothing, that stray man would then pack up a horse with his bedroll, throw his mount of horses in with his cattle and start for the home ranch which might be several days away. He would usually plan to strike ranches on the way home so as to have a place to pen his cattle and to eat and bunk for the night. In the main herd cutting continued till every stray man working on the roundup had gotten his own cattle and left.

After the work, there probably would be a few head of strays left which nobody claimed. These were put into a corral and roped in order to determine the brand more readily. If the ownership were in doubt due to the illegibility of the brand, the hair was picked, pulled out, or clipped. The rightful owner was then notified, and meanwhile these strays were held in a pasture. If the owner lived too far away to make it worth his while to come after them, he would notify the ranch to include them in the first shipment and sell them, remitting the money to him. Nowadays, an inspector of the Cattle Sanitary Board takes charge of such cattle. But in the old days thanks to good will among owners very little stray stock was lost.

As soon as the calf roundup was over, the chuck wagon was pulled up to the ranch house and unloaded. The hands at this time usually took a day or so off, going to town to do any necessary trading—in either dry and wet goods.

A Bibliography of the New Mexico Cattle Frontier

Adams, Ramon F. *The Rampaging Herd*. University of Oklahoma Press, 1959.

Alvis, Berry Newton. "History of Union County, New Mexico." New Mexico Historical Review. Vol. 22, no. 3, July, 1947.

Athern, Robert G. *Westward the Briton*. New York: Charles Scribner's Sons, 1953.

Atherton, Lewis E. *The Cattle Kings*. Bloomington: Indiana University Press, 1961.

Armstrong, Ruth W. *The Chases of Cimarron*. Albuquerque: New Mexico Stockman, 1981.

Baydo, Gerald R. *Cattle Ranching in Territorial New Mexico*. Unpublished Doctoral dissertation. University of New Mexico, 1970.

Branch, Douglas. *The Cowboy and His Interpreters*. New York: Cooper Square Publishers, 1961.

Burroughs, Jean. *On the Trail: The Life and Tales of Lead Steer Potter*. Santa Fe: Museum of New Mexico Press, 1980.

Caffey, David L. *Chasing the Santa Fe Ring*. Albuquerque: University of New Mexico Press, 2015.

Caffey, David L. *Frank Springer and New Mexico*. College Station: Texas A&M University Press, 2007.

Chase, C.M. *The Editor,s Run in New Mexico and Colorado*. Ft. Davis: Frontier Book Company, 1968.

Culley, John H. *Cattle, Horses, and Men of the Western Ranges*. Tucson: University of Arizona Press, 1985.

Clarke, Mary W. *John Chisum: Jinglebob King of Texas*. Austin: Eakins Press, 1984.

Cleaveland, Agnes Morley. *No Life for a Lady*. Boston: Houghton Mifflin, 1941.

Coe, Wilbur C. *Ranch on the Ruidoso*. New York: Alfred A. Knopf, 1968.

Cook, James A. *Fifty Years on the Old Frontier*. Norman: University of Oklahoma Press, 1954.

Cramer, Dudley T. *The Pecos Ranchers in the Lincoln County War*. Oakland: Branding Iron Press, 1996.

Curry, George. *George Curry*. Albuquerque: University of New Mexico Press, 1958.

Dale, Everett E. *The Range Cattle Industry*. Norman: University of Oklahoma Press, 1930.

Dobie, J. Frank. *The Longhorns*. New York: Grossett & Dunlap, 1941.

Foster, Mark S. *Henry M. Porter*. Niwot: University of Colorado Press, 1991.

Freeman, James W. *Prose and Poetry of the Livestock Industry of the United States*. New York: Antiquarian Press, 1959.

French, William. *Some Recollections of a Western Ranchman*. Silver City: High Lonesome Press, 1997.

Frink, Maurice, W. Turrentine Jackson, and Agnes Wright Spring. *When Grass was King*. Boulder: University of Colorado Press, 1956.

Gressley, Gene M. *Bankers and Cattlemen*. Lincoln: University of Nebraska Press, 1971.

Haley, J. Evetts. *Charles Goodnight, Cowman and Plainsman*. Norman: University of Oklahoma Press, 1949.

Haley, J. Evetts. *George W. Littlefield, Texan*. Norman: University of Oklahoma Press, 1943.

Hinkle, James F. *Early Days of a Cowboy on the Pecos*. Santa Fe: Stagecoach Press, 1965.

Hinton, Harwood P. "John Simpson Chisum, 1877–1884." New Mexico Historical Review, XXXI, July, 1956, XXXI, October, 1956, XXXIII, January, 1957.

Horgan, Paul. *Great River: The Rio Grande in North American History*. 2 vols. New York: Holt, Rinehart and Winston, 1954.

Hunter, J. Marvin. *The Trail Drivers of Texas*. Austin: University of Texas Press, 1985.

Hutchison, W.H. *A Bar Cross Man: The Life and Personal Writings of Eugene Manlove Rhodes*. Norman: University of Oklahoma Press, 1956.

Keleher, William A. *Maxwell Land Grant: A New Mexico Item*. Santa Fe: Sunstone Press, 2008.

Keleher, William A. *The Fabulous Frontier*. Santa Fe: Sunstone Press, 2008.

Maddux, Vernon R. *John Hittson*. Niwot: University of Colorado Press, 1994.

McCoy, Joseph. *Historic Sketches of the Cattle Trade*. Lincoln: University of Nebraska Press, 1985.

McDonald, Jerry. *Sequential Land Use of the Philmont Scout Ranch Region, Northeastern New Mexico*. Unpublished Master's thesis. University of Texas, 1972.

Miller, Darlis. *Open Range*. Norman: University of Oklahoma Press, 2011.

Muir, Emma M. "Pioneer Ranch," New Mexico Magazine, XXXVI, June, 1958.

Murphy, Lawrence R. *Lucien Maxwell: Bonaparte of the West*. Norman: University of Oklahoma Press, 1983.

Murphy, Lawrence R. *Philmont: A History of New Mexico's Cimarron Country*. Albuquerque: University of New Mexico Press, 1972.

Noel, Leon. "The Largest Estate in the World." Overland Monthly. XII, November, 1888.

Oden, B.A. *Early Days on the Texas-New Mexico Plains*. Canyon: Palo Duro Press, 1965.

Osgood, Ernest Staples. *The Day of the Cattleman*. Chicago: University of Chicago Press, 1957.

Patterson, Paul E. and Joy Poole. *Great Plains Cattle Empire*. Lubbock: Texas Tech University Press, 2000.

Paxson, Frederic L. "The Cow Country." American Historical Review, XXII, Oct.-July, 1917.

Pearson, Jim Berry. *The Maxwell Land Grant*. Norman: University of Oklahoma Press, 1961.

Potter, Jack. *Cattle Trails of the Old West*. Clayton: Leader Press, 1935.

Potter, Jack. *Lead Steer*. Clayton: Leader Press, 1939.

Remley, David A. *Bell Ranch: Cattle Ranching in the Southwest, 1824–1947*. Albuquerque: University of New Mexico Press, 1993.

Rhodes, Eugene Manlove. *West is West*. New York: Grosett & Dunlap, 1917.

Rhodes, May Davison. *The Hired Man on Horseback*. Boston: Houghton Mifflin Company, 1938.

Seton, Ernest Thompson. *Trail of an Artist-Naturalist*. New York: Charles Scribner's Sons, 1940.

Sherrow, James E. *The Chisholm Trail*. Norman: University of Oklahoma Press, 2018.

Sonnichsen, C.L. *Tularosa*. Albuquerque: University of New Mexico Press, 1980.

Stanley, F. "New Mexico's Fabulous Dorsey." New Mexico Historical Review, XXV, June, 1958.

Stevens, Montague. *Meet Mr. Grizzly*. Albuquerque: University of New Mexico Press, 1943.

Taylor, Morris F. "The Maxwell Cattle Company, 1881–1888." New Mexico Historical Review. XXXXIX, October, 1974.

Taylor, Morris F. "Stephen Dorsey, Speculator-Cattleman." New Mexico Historical Society. XXXXIX, January, 1974.

Thompson, Albert W. *They Were Open Range Days*. Denver: World Press Company, 1946.

Thorp, N. Howard (Jack). *Pardner of the Wind*. Lincoln: University of Nebraska Press, 1977.

Thorp, N. Howard (Jack). *Songs of the Cowboys*. Lincoln: University of Nebraska Press, 1985.

Von Richthofen, Walter Baron. *Cattle Raising on the Plains of North America*. Norman: University of Oklahoma Press, 1964.

Wallis, George A. *Cattle Kings of the Staked Plains*. Denver: Sage Press, 1957.

Webb, Walter Prescott. *The Great Plains*. Lincoln: University of Nebraska Press, 1981.

Wellman, Paul. *The Trampling Herd*. New York: Doubleday & Company, 1951.

Westermier, Clifford P. *Trailing the Cowboy*. Caldwell: The Caxton Printers, 1955.

Westphal, Victor. *The Public Domain in New Mexico, 1854–1891*. Albuquerque: University of New Mexico Press, 1965.

Westphal, Victor. *Thomas Benton Catron and His Era*. Tucson: University of Arizona Press, 1973.

White, Peter and Mary Ann White. *Along the Rio Grande*. Santa Fe: Ancient City Press, 1988.

Whitlock, Vivan H. *Cowboy Life on the Llano Estacado*. Norman: University of Oklahoma Press, 1970.

Williams, Jerry L. *New Mexico in Maps*. Albuquerque: University of New Mexico Press, 1986.

Willoughby, Roy. *The Range Cattle Industry of New Mexico*. Unpublished Master's thesis. University of New Mexico, 1933.

Woods, Lawrence M. *British Gentlemen in the Wild West*. New York: The Free Press, 1989.

CPSIA information can be obtained
at www.ICGtesting.com
Printed in the USA
BVHW080306040123
655462BV00003B/530